TEN

Exciting *Historic Sites*

to Visit in Upstate New York

DAVID MACNAB

PAGE PUBLISHING, INC.
New York, NY

First originally published by Page Publishing, Inc. 2016

ISBN 978-1-68409-280-2 (Paperback)
ISBN 978-1-68409-281-9 (Digital)

Printed in the United States of America

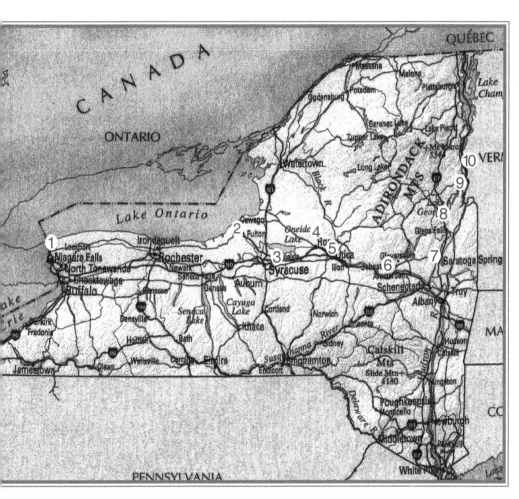

Map from US Government (http:/NationalMap.gov)

KEY TO MAP

1. Old Fort Niagara
2. Fort Ontario at Oswego
3. Erie Canal State Historic Park
4. Fort Stanwix National Monument
5. Oriskany Battlefield State Historic Site
6. Johnson Hall State Historic Site
7. Fort William Henry Museum
8. Saratoga Battlefield National Historical Park
9. Fort Ticonderoga
10. British Fort at Crown Point

Contents

Acknowledgments 9

Introduction... 11

"Old" Fort Niagara 21

Fort Ontario 31

Old Erie Canal 39

Fort Stanwix 47

Oriskany Battlefield.. 57

Johnson Hall 67

Fort William Henry Museum and Restoration 75

Saratoga Battlefield National Historical Park 85

Fort Ticonderoga.. 97

Crown Point State Historic Site 107

Sources... 117

Index.. 125

To my sister Katherine Wylie
Whose generous spirit, encouragement, and smart ideas
have helped make several dream projects possible

Acknowledgments

I would like to acknowledge the significant help and encouragement that I have received, from a number of people, while working on this project. Hopefully people realize that a positive attitude and encouragement can have a surprisingly significant impact on others.

My sister, Katherine Wylie, has been extremely helpful with her great ideas, interest, and support. Barbara Hunt has been a great help with her skillful typing, significant grammatical corrections, suggestions, and encouragement. Countless times Dr. Brandon Beck, my lifelong friend, has supplied great advice and encouragement. Sharing his wisdom as a respected history professor and successful author has been invaluable. S. J. Coniglio has been a constant help with his interest, ideas, wisdom, encouragement, proofreading, suggestions, photos, and opinions.

The United States National Park Service, with their on-site rangers, is an important agency that protects our precious national heritage sites and enhances our visits to them. People at this agency have been extremely helpful to this project by supplying factual data as well as guidance and permission to use some of their beautiful digital images. The wonderful rangers at Fort Stanwix (William Sawyer, Kelly Roman), Battle of Oriskany State Historic site, and Saratoga Battlefield (Gina Johnson) have been particularly helpful. Melodie Viele at Fort William Henry was a delight by supplying information and a welcoming attitude. Fort Ticonderoga Museum's Christopher Fox supplied a terrific photo.

John Stanton, a great photographer and a contributor to FortWiki.com, once again, generously shared some of his wonderful photos. Carl Heilman II allowed the use of two of his beautiful photos.

Other people who helped this project materially and with their ideas and encouragement are Mike Kurdziel, Peter Rich, Lyndie Smith, Matt Johnson, Walter and Shirley Johnson.

Introduction

Early American History is interesting and exciting. Visiting historic sites can be fun and even thrilling. The joy a historic site can provide is significantly enhanced if the visitor has some knowledge of the history of the site before visiting. Upstate New York is rich in important and exciting colonial era (and later) historic sites. These are the underlying concepts behind this book. We will first present descriptive and logistic information regarding ten very interesting Upstate New York historic sites that provide facilities for visitors (these sites will be roughly near or above the middle of the state; their location thus qualifying for the designation as "upstate"). Next we will present a detailed, though brief, history of each site, enabling the reader to maximize their enjoyment while visiting the site. In addition, we will provide driving directions and site contact information. Some sites in New York are not open all year round, so we will include times of the year when the site is open and hours of operation. Finally, we will include our sources to help readers who are interested in pursuing more details about the sites and the historic times that spawned them.

At one time or another, most of us have had a thought that goes something like "I wonder what it was like to live in those times" or "what did it feel like to be there at that time?" Visiting a historic site can give us live mental images to put with our intellectual understanding of the site. This way, visiting an historic site can help us experience what it looked like to be there in the past, and even help us to "feel" what it was like to be there. As a result, we have a more complete understanding of a historic event, or location, than if we just read about it or had seen it on television. Since individually, and as a people, we are all products of our history, historic sites are very important to our collective soul as a nation.

Some of the most interesting aspects of history are the connections between then and now, facets of people's lives in the past, that we can identify with now. People in the past had to find ways to procure food, cloth themselves, and provide shelter from the elements, just as we need to do today. Visiting historic sites can show us what they ate, how they obtained their food, how they dressed, and what their homes looked like. Similarly we can see how people travelled, earned a living, fought the inevitable wars, and even how they related to each other. It is possible that understanding our history a little more clearly can help us better understand our present.

SOME TERMS AND CONVENTIONS USED IN THIS BOOK

For simplicity, whenever we say New York State we will mean the area encompassed by the current boundaries of New York State even when speaking of times before New York became a state in the year 1777. The same convention will apply to other states as well as Canada.

Terms of political affiliation can be confusing especially when speaking about the American Revolutionary War. This war was hardly a unanimous decision on the part of rebelling colonials. Many colonial citizens remained loyal to the British king and wanted to remain colonists of Great Britain. These people were known as Tories or Loyalists. Colonists in favor of independence from England were called Patriots, Whigs, Americans, or sometimes Continentals (i.e., General George Washington's Continental Army).

Defining a few military terms may also be useful. Militia refers to men who go about their lives as private citizens until "called out" because of some type of emergency at which time they form quasi-military units and behave as soldiers. Most militia units were Patriots. Regular army (or Regulars) refers to men who are full-time professional soldiers. There were British Regulars and Continental (Patriot) Regulars.

AN UNDERLYING CONFLICT

It is useful to understand something about the times in which historic events occur in order to help us see why they unfolded the way they did. Much of North American history during the latter half of the seventeenth century and first two-thirds of the eighteenth century was a result of the struggle between France and England for control of that area. For most of this period the French inhabited the region along the banks of the St. Lawrence River, and they later expanded west and south down the Ohio and Mississippi Rivers. Meanwhile the English were settling along the Atlantic Coast as far west as the Appalachian Mountains.

The French approach to colonization in North America differed markedly from that of the English. The French were primarily interested in exploiting the fur trade (an extremely important economic resource throughout the period) whereas the English were clearing and settling on the land for agricultural reasons, creating farms. The English also harvested timber fairly extensively. One result of these two differing cultural approaches was that the North American Natives tended to gravitate more to the French than the English, since there was little interest on the part of the French to disenfranchise the Indians from their land.

The manifestation of the conflict between these two world powers was a series of wars fought between England and France called the French and Indian Wars. The last of these wars was called the French and Indian War (in Europe it was called the Seven Years' War), fought between 1755 and 1763. The English won this war, much of which was fought in the area encompassed by the current New York State. The Treaty of Paris signed in 1763 resulted in France giving up most of its land claims in North America.

To get a feeling of the turbulent time period we are interested in, we present a list of wars that affected North American and New York State history, along with the years in which they were fought.

1. King Phillip's War (1675–1678). Featured the Wampanoag Indians led by Metacomet (King Phillip) rising up against encroachment by English settlers.

2. King William's War (1688–1697). This was the first of four French and Indian wars.

3. Queen Anne's War (1702–1713). The second French and Indian War and of similar nature to King William's war in that the French and their Wabanaki allies conducted raids against English settlements as part of a larger war in Europe.

4. King George's War (1744–1748). This was the so-called third French and Indian war. Again a European war with collateral effects in North America.

5. French and Indian War (1754–1763). Also known as the Seven Years' War. This was the greatest and last French and Indian war. It ended with France relinquishing her territory in North America to England. Much of this war was fought in New York State.

6. American Revolution (1774–1783). New York State was the site of a number of crucial history altering battles during this war.

7. War of 1812 (1812–1815). Between Great Britain and the young United States as Britain was attacking US merchant shipping and impressing American sailors into the British Navy.

8. American Civil War (1861–1865). No actual fighting occurred in New York.

UPSTATE NEW YORK HISTORY - PRE-EUROPEAN CONTACT

The area now encompassed by New York State has long played (and continues to play) a prominent role in the history of North America. The first inhabitants of New York arrived here about ten thousand years ago. Although there is a lack of consensus among archeologists and anthropologists, it is a decent probability that these early Native Americans were descendants of even earlier people who arrived in North America by crossing a land bridge from northern Asia. Some sources suggest that by around AD 800 the ancestors of the Iroquois (a family of tribes who are related to each other by sharing a similar language structure [Iroquoian]) had moved into the New York State area from the Appalachian region to the south. (Some sources also suggest that some of the Iroquois came from the Saint Lawrence River area in the late 1500s.) During the same periods some members of another family of Native groups, the Algonquians (i.e., Mohicans), were beginning to arrive along the upper Hudson River area. By AD 1000, the Native American territories were quite well established in the areas where the early European travelers would find them. Most of New York State was the territory of various Iroquois tribes, while the Hudson River area and east was the territory of various Algonquian peoples. Whether Iroquoian or Algonquian, most of these tribes subsisted by growing corn, squash, and beans, and by hunting deer, bear, moose, and other animals. There seems to have been a great deal of inter-tribal warfare between the two main groups mentioned, and also between tribes within the groups.

The warfare between tribes within the Iroquois group was finally recognized as being very self-destructive and steps were taken to improve the situation. No one is certain exactly when the "non-aggression" Iroquois Confederacy (or league) was formed, but many sources put the date somewhere around 1570 (another possible date is 1451). Also there were other Iroquoian confederacies formed at one time or another, for example the Huron. All of these confederacies were formed before European contact, and while fairly sophisticated, there was one main tenet. The tribes within the Iroquois confederacy (in fact all confederacies) would not attack and kill each other. The Iroquoian tribes who joined Iroquois confederacy were the Seneca, Cayuga, Onondaga, Oneida, and Mohawk. Later, early in the eighteenth century (possibly the year 1714), a sixth tribe, the Tuscarora, was given a somewhat limited membership.

Although each member of the league was free to pursue their own wars and politics, the strength gained by not attacking each other was immense, and the Iroquois League became the strongest Native American group in eastern North America. This was the situation that the Europeans began to encounter as they expanded west from the Atlantic coast into New York and beyond.

EARLY EUROPEANS IN NEW YORK

Waterways have always been the primary avenue for exploration of new lands, and early New York exploration is no exception. In 1524, Giovanni de Verrazano sailed through the Narrows and into New York Bay. Verrazano was an Italian sailor in the employ of the king of France. He sailed around the mouth of the Hudson River and actually landed on Manhattan Island. The next year a Spanish expedition led by Portuguese captain Esteban Gomez sailed a short distance up the Hudson River. In spite of glowing reports of their findings, Gomez and Verrazano were the last, as far as is known, explorers to travel up the Hudson River during the sixteenth century, although a French expedition from the north, established a short-lived trading post at the future site of Albany in 1540.

The next significant European to enter the New York State area was a Frenchman, Samuel De Champlain. Champlain had been exploring the St. Laurence River region of what would become Canada. In July 1609, Champlain and several other Frenchmen, along with their harquebus (matchlock muskets), accompanied an Algonquian War party heading south along the shore of what would become Lake Champlain. As they approached the south end of the Lake they encountered a Mohawk war party just offshore of the Ticonderoga Peninsula. After spending the night preparing themselves a battle ensued. This resulted in a victory for the Algonquians, aided greatly by the Frenchmen and their guns. The Iroquois never completely forgave the French for this action.

The same year, 1609, an English explorer, employed by the Dutch East India Company, sailed into New York Bay and then up the river later named for him. Henry Hudson took ten days to sail his ship, the Halve Maen, up the river to present-day Albany. Along the way the ship traded with several native groups and obtained a quantity of furs. As a result of Hudson's voyage, the Dutch claimed this region as their own, and in 1614 they established a trading post in the Albany area (Castle Island) and named it Fort Nassau. In 1617 this fort was flooded out, leading to the construction of Fort Orange nearby (in an area less susceptible to flooding). At the same time the Dutch were also establishing a presence on present-day Manhattan

Island, which they named New Amsterdam. Unfortunately for them, the English conquered New Netherland (the territory from present New York to Albany) in 1664 and renamed the colony and the city New York. At that time the European population of New York was seven thousand to eight thousand.

New Netherland was now New York Province and began a period of steady expansion as such for more than 110 years, until it became New York State in 1777. Throughout this period the New York economy featured large manorial estates producing grain for consumption and trade. In addition, lumber was an important product, especially for trade with the British sugar colonies.

FRENCH AND INDIAN WAR

Throughout the late seventeenth century and more than half of the eighteenth century, there was a series of conflicts, between France and England for control of North America. These wars are often called the French and Indian Wars, and culminated with **The** French and Indian War from 1755–1763. New York was a focal point for this war, as major critical battles were fought at Fort Niagara, Oswego, and around Lakes George and Champlain. A feature of these wars was the use of Native American allies on both sides. The Iroquois, who hated the French, tended to help the English, while various Algonquian tribes (and some Iroquoian as well, i.e., the Huron) aided the French. The struggle between the two great European powers for control of North America virtually ended when England defeated the French at Quebec in 1760 (although the official end of the war did not occur until 1763 with the signing of the Treaty of Paris).

THE REVOLUTIONARY WAR

New York State played a crucial role in the American Revolutionary War. Although much of the war was played out in the New York City to Philadelphia area, Upstate New York was the scene of a number of crucial battles. In fact, two of the most important battles in the history of the world were fought just north of Albany. The battles of

Saratoga proved to the colonials, and the world, that the American Continental Army could beat the best-equipped and best-trained regular army in the world, that of the British. The victory of the colonials over General Burgoyne at Saratoga encouraged France to come to the aid of the Americans. Without the help of France it is doubtful that the Americans could have won their freedom. It is ironic that while General Horatio Gates is given credit for the American victory at Saratoga, General Benedict Arnold (the later traitor) played a crucial role in winning the battle for the Americans.

THE EARLY NINETEENTH CENTURY AND THE ERIE CANAL

After the Revolutionary War, Upstate New York continued to expand in a westerly direction, influenced greatly by advances in transportation. In 1807 Robert Fulton began a steamboat line that ran from New York City to Albany. This was the first successful steamboat enterprise in North America. By 1815 the steady western migration enabled Albany to become a turnpike hub for pioneers heading for Buffalo and other points west. However, the biggest transportation development was the opening of the Erie Canal in 1825.

It would be almost impossible to overestimate the impact that the building of the Erie Canal had on the development of New York State. The idea for building such a canal was first voiced by a flour merchant named Jesse Hawley in the early 1790s. After much skepticism about the viability of the project, the New York State legislature finally funded it, and construction of the canal began in 1817. It was completed in 1825. The finished canal reflected the vision and political clout of then New York governor Clinton and was sometimes called Clinton's folly. It ran 363 miles from Buffalo to Albany and was forty feet wide and four feet deep. Boats on the canal were primarily moved by means of being towed by a horse, or mule which was walking along the adjacent tow path.

The Erie Canal is considered the engineering marvel of the nineteenth century. Even more amazing than its construction is the economic impact the canal had on New York State and New York

City. One measure of this impact of the canal on the state can be gleaned by looking at a map of New York. Every sizable city in this state except Elmira and Binghamton is located along the corridor created by the canal and its connection to the ocean, the Hudson River. Eighty percent of the population of Upstate New York lives within twenty-five miles of the canal.

The canal fostered agricultural development in the state by giving farmers a cheap way to ship their produce, especially wheat, to New York City and hence the world. As early as 1834 the cost of the canal had been recouped from the tolls. By 1840 New York City had become the busiest port in America, outshipping Boston, Baltimore, and New Orleans combined. In 1841, more than one million bushels of wheat were transported on the canal. This incredible economic success continued on for the rest of the nineteenth century and well into the twentieth century. Between 1905 and 1918 the Erie Canal was enlarged several times to accommodate bigger barges, and much of the original channel was abandoned. By the 1940s railroads and highways competed strongly for the transport business, and traffic on the canal system declined dramatically. Thankfully there are a number of places (see chapter 3) where visitors can view original locks and even a portion of the original channel of the wonderful Erie Canal.

GET OUT AND VISIT A NEW YORK STATE HISTORIC SITE

By now it should be clear that New York State is incredibly rich in early American history. In fact a case can easily be made that New York has the most exciting historic sites in the United States. To get the most out of a visit to a historic site you should prepare ahead of your visit. Make sure the site is open when you plan to visit and be sure that you have solid directions to get you there. Most of all familiarize yourself with the history of the site before you go (read the chapter covering that site) as this will make a huge difference in your enjoyment level. Don't be afraid to let yourself be excited by some of New York's fabulous historic sites.

I.

"Old" Fort Niagara

State Historic Site

The Castle at "Old" Fort Niagara (Photo courtesy S. J. Coniglio)

Location: Fort Niagara State Park, Youngstown, NY

Directions: From Niagara Falls, USA. Take Robert Moses Parkway North. From Niagara Falls, Canada. Cross either Lewiston Queenstown or Rainbow Bridges and take Robert Moses Parkway North.

From New York State Thruway. Exit 50 follow I-290 West to I-190 North. Exit 25B to Robert Moses Parkway North

Coordinates: 43,262691 N, -79.063314 W

Season: All year. Closed Jan 1, Thanksgiving, December 25. 9:00 am to 5:00 pm every day except 9:00 am to 7:00 pm July, August. Last admission is one-half hour before close.

Admission: Moderate fee (under 6 free). Discount for either Senior Citizen, AAA member, NYS Parks Master Pass coupon, guests of Old Fort Niagara association members.

Contact: PO Box 169, Youngstown, NY 14174-0169

Phone: (716)745-7611

Web: http://www.nysparks.com/historic-sites/31/details.aspx

DESCRIPTION

"Old" Fort Niagara is a thirty-acre complex of eighteenth century stone buildings, redoubts (supporting mini-forts), and earthworks located on the south shore of Lake Ontario. The fort rests on a point of land where the Niagara River enters the southwest corner of the lake. It is one of the most interesting and important historic sites in North America. There are a number of impressive fortification works (defensive earthworks and bastions) which were constructed at various times over the years depending on who was in control of the fort: the French, the English, or the Americans. The fort is surrounded by brick ramparts (defensive wall). In front of the land side rampart is a large triangular defensive fortification called a ravelin, and in front of the ravelin's southeast wall is a smaller fortification called a demi-lune. Inside the fort and spaced around the large central open grassy area are six stone buildings; all are original, as constructed in the 1700s.

Dominating everything is the two-and-one-half-story rectangular stone chateau, sometimes referred to as the "Castle." It was designed by a Frenchman, Chaussegros de Lery, to be a self-contained fortress that looks like a peaceful trading house. This impressive building was built in 1726–1727. The reason it was intended to appear only as a trading house rather than a military post was to ease the objections of the Iroquois Indians to its presence. The chateau measures ninety-six feet by forty-eight feet and has a double-pitched hip roof. The construction is of un-coursed field stone, with the window and doorway trims made of cut bluestone. Inside the chateau are a large trading room, troop billets, a powder magazine, a provisions storehouse, a bakery, a kitchen, a chapel, officers' quarters, and the commandant's quarters and office. Visitors may walk throughout the Castle and experience what it would have felt like to be there in the 1700s.

In addition to the chateau there are five other original stone buildings inside the ramparts. Two of these are the north and south redoubts (two-story mini-forts) located in the northeast and southeast corners of the fort. The other original buildings are a storehouse, a powder magazine, and a bake house.

Visitors enter the fort through a drawbridge on the south side, and once inside are facing the south redoubt. After entering the fort and turning to the left, a visitor would approach a long stone building that was used as a provisions storehouse. This building serves to display some interesting artifacts of the fort's early times. At a right angle to the far end of the storehouse is the powder magazine (built in 1757), which visitors may enter. Moving farther northwest the visitor encounters a log building (not original) where refreshments are sold. Moving along the rampart and turning north the visitor comes upon the interesting stone bake house (built in 1762) with a nice display of its functionality inside. The bake house is at the southwest corner of the chateau.

To enhance the visitor experience some of the staff of Fort Niagara dress in very authentic period clothing and accoutrements. Also, there are daily (sometimes hourly) demonstrations of the care and firing of the British musket of the day, the fabled Brown Bess. In addition the fort has a number of special events intended to demonstrate various aspects of life at the fort in the eighteenth century. Visitors should check the Web site to see a schedule of upcoming events (and a description of them) or call the fort for that information. Finally, there is a very nice gift shop at the entrance/exit to the site.

BRIEF HISTORY

GEOGRAPHY AND EARLY HISTORY

Geography has always been very important, especially when talking about the advance of civilization. The piece of land upon which Old Fort Niagara is found has been geographically important to people for a very long time. The fort sits on a triangular piece of land (characterized by high bluffs) on the east bank of the Niagara River exactly where it enters the southwest corner of Lake Ontario. The Niagara River flows out of Lake Eire and empties into Lake Ontario, which eventually flows into the St. Lawrence River which, of course, flows farther eastward into the North Atlantic Ocean. This path in reverse is the road which leads from the Atlantic Coast to the upper great lakes and the heart of North America. This critical route depended on a portage along the Niagara River, since Niagara Falls is obviously impassable. A fort along this route could (and did) control access to the interior of the continent.

Archeological evidence indicates that the area around the mouth of the Niagara River has been inhabited by Indians for at least ten thousand years. The evidence suggests that this Indian presence was in the form of small seasonal or temporary camps. By the time of the first European contact (the early 1600s) the Niagara route to the interior had been heavily travelled by Indians for a very long time and was then the territory of the Seneca Indians (a member of the Iroquois Confederacy).

It is hard to overestimate the importance of the fur trade between the Indians and the Europeans during the seventeenth and eighteenth centuries. As a result of this trade, the Europeans received the wealth-producing furs, and the Indians received items that soon became necessities to them, such as metal items like cooking pots, knifes, fish hooks, as well as clothing and beads, and eventually firearms. Each side of these trading transactions highly valued the items they received. The fur trade was so big that the fur-bearing animals became trapped out in the east, forcing the Indians to obtain their furs from the more western areas. Much of this trade was funneled through the Niagara portage, with furs coming east and people and supplies heading west.

The first European to recognize the strategic importance of the mouth of the Niagara River was the French explorer LaSalle. LaSalle had a wooden fort built on the site in 1679 as part of his plans to explore the Mississippi River basin. Later that year the Indians destroyed the fort, which had been called Fort Conti. In 1687 the French governor, Denonville, built a much larger wooden fort on the same site called Fort Denonville. This fort was garrisoned with one hundred men. However, most of the men died over the winter and the fort was abandoned.

BIRTH OF FORT NIAGARA

Finally in 1725 the French began construction, on the same site as the two previous forts, of a much more substantial stone fort, to be called Fort Niagara. Although Fort Niagara was conceived in order to militarily control the important route to the Great Lakes Region, the main building (the Castle) was designed to look like a trading house. This was in order to quell the reluctance of the Seneca Indians to allow the presence of a fort on this site. The stone chateau was designed by the famous French architect Chaussegros de Lery. Extensive defensive earthworks around the fort were implemented at the same time as the chateau was constructed.

Over the years, depending on which country controlled the fort, the defensive earthworks and some of the buildings were updated and other buildings added. In 1757 the outer defenses of the fort were expanded by French Captain Pouchot. As part of that expansion, the large stone powder magazine was built.

During the French and Indian War, the fort changed hands from the French to the British after a siege in 1759. The stone bake house was added in 1762 by the British to replace the old one, which was destroyed during that siege. The stone storehouse was built just prior to the war of 1812 by the British in the same area where the French storehouse had been. This same period of British habitation of the fort (late eighteenth and early nineteenth centuries) produced the north and south redoubts. Finally, some of the fort's substantial earthworks were built during the Civil War, and at the same locations as the French earthworks had been.

LIFE AND EVENTS AT THE FORT

Fort Niagara's mission was to protect and control the vital route to the huge Great Lakes Basin and to serve as an important trading post for the fur trade. In the beginning this enabled the French to control much of the fur trade as well as provide a supply post for their forts in the Ohio Country.

The liveliest and most important period or Fort Niagara's long existence is from 1726 to 1816. The fort was then a hub of activity, much of it occurring between the west wall and the river, in an area called the bottoms. This area is now occupied by a Coast Guard Station, but back in the aforementioned period, there was an extensive trader town in this area, dependent on the fort. Archeological excavations have confirmed the existence of the trader town, and it is believed that there were over fifty buildings in this area. They included warehouses, taverns, commercial buildings, row houses, docks, wharfs, and boathouses.

FORT NIAGARA DURING
THE FRENCH AND INDIAN WAR

We have seen that Fort Niagara was built by the French in order to control a strategic route to the interior of America. The French also used the fort to supply a string of forts in the Ohio country. With

26

the outbreak of the French and Indian War between the French and English for control of North America, the fort became strategically crucial. The war began in 1755, at which time the French commandant of the fort was a Captain Pouchot. Pouchot knew he would be attacked by the English at some point, so he expanded the fort's fortifications in 1757. This included the construction of the large separate stone powder magazine.

Captain Pouchot was correct in his belief that he would be attacked. In July 1759 a large British force arrived in front of the fort under the command of Brigadier General John Prideaux. Prideaux's forces numbered three thousand soldiers and about six hundred Iroquois warriors (led by provincial officer Sir William Johnson). On July 6, 1759, the British began siege operations against the fort. Inside the fort, Captain Pouchot commanded about two hundred regular troops, twenty artillerymen, three hundred Canadian provincials, and about one hundred friendly Iroquois (who, unfortunately for the French, departed when the British arrived).

The French strongly defended the fort against the siege, but they were badly outnumbered and under constant bombardment. Captain Pouchot sent for help to the French Fort Machault, which was to the south. In the meantime, the English General Prideaux was killed by one of his own cannons and Sir William Johnson assumed the British command.

The French relief forces from the Fort Machault were led by Captain Lignery. On July 24, about two miles from Fort Niagara, Lignery and his men were ambushed by English regulars and Iroquois warriors, and routed. This debacle for the French is called the Battle of La Belle-Famille (the name of a clearing where the battle was fought). Learning that his relief column would never arrive, Captain Pouchot surrendered Fort Niagara to the British on July 26, 1759. In September 1760, the French surrendered all their North American territory to the British (although the treaty ending the war was not officially signed until 1763).

BRITISH OCCUPATION

During the English occupation (after 1759), the fort was used for the fur trade and as a military installation. After 1775 it became an important post from which the British launched terroristic raids against American settlements as part of the Revolutionary War. Even after America won the war in 1783, the British kept possession of Fort Niagara.

AMERICAN OCCUPATION

Finally in 1796 the British relinquished control of the Fort Niagara to the United States. American control of Fort Niagara did not last long. On December 19, 1813, during the War of 1812, the British recaptured the fort. However, as a result of the US victory in that war in 1815, the British returned the fort to the United States, for good this time.

MILITARY IMPORTANCE OF FORT NIAGARA LESSENS

After the War of 1812 ended, the military importance of Fort Niagara was greatly diminished although it continued to serve as a military base for more than a century. In 1825 the Erie Canal opened along its entire length from Buffalo to Albany, and thus connecting to the Hudson River and New York City. This greatly diminished the economic importance of the fort at the same time that the center of fur trade had shifted much farther west. Fort Niagara had become unnecessary.

During the Civil War, some enhancements were made to the fort just in case the Canadians wanted to assist the Confederates. During World War I the fort was used for training and processing American troops on their way to Europe. Fort Niagara was put to the same use during World War II and also served as a POW camp. In 1945 Fort Niagara was turned over to the Niagara Frontier State Parks Commission.

Though we are now in the twenty-first century, visitors making an unforgettable trip to the fort at the mouth of the Niagara River will find that it is easy to visualize French, British, or American soldiers, Native Americans, and fur traders walking across the central grounds toward the Castle or to see fur-laden canoes pulling up along the Bottoms just outside the walls of fabulous "Old" Fort Niagara.

II.

Fort Ontario

State Historic Site

Central part of Fort Ontario (Photo courtesy
John Stanton of FortWiki.com)

Location: 1 East Fourth Street Oswego, New York, 13126

Directions: From the west take Route NY 104 east to Oswego and
turn left on East Fourth Street. If approaching from east, East
Fourth Street will be on your right.

GPS Coordinates: 43.465833 N, – 76.508056 W

Season: Mid-May through Mid-October.

Open May to June, Wednesday through Sunday
10:00 am – 4:30 pm

Open July to September 2, Daily 10:00 am – 4:30 pm

September 4 – Mid-October, Wednesday – Sunday
10:00 am – 4:30 pm

Admission: Small fee charged
Contact: Friends at Fort Ontario, PO Box 5379, Oswego, NY 13126
(315)343-4711
Web: http://www.nysparks.com/historic-sites/20/details.aspx

DESCRIPTION

Today's Fort Ontario State Historic Site preserves a mid-nineteenth century American fort situated on a very historical piece of land. The area where the fort is located, on the northeast side of the Oswego River where it empties into Lake Ontario, has been an important strategic location for many centuries. The current Fort Ontario is actually the fourth fort to be built on this site. It is a star-shaped stone-walled fort with five sides and with bastions (pointed projections allowing defenders to fire parallel to the walls) on each point. It was built between 1838 and 1844 and includes some improvements made from 1863 to 1872.

The interior of the fort features a central round grass parade ground surrounded by a slightly oval road and a number of interesting structures between the road and the walls of the fort. The interior structures are two stone officers' barracks, two guardhouses, a powder magazine, a storehouse, and an enlisted men's barracks.

Officer's quarters number one is a three-story stone building erected between 1842 and 1844. The first and second floors of the barracks were used as two six-room apartments for officers and their families. The third floor was occupied by servants. There are two smaller wooden structures on either side of the main building which were used for storage and a privy. Around 1870 this officers' quarter was occupied by Lieutenant Colonel Robert L. Kirkpatrick, First Lieutenant Michael J. Hogarty, and their families.

A powder magazine is situated along the eastern portion of the central road. Next in line, along the southern portion of the interior, is the enlisted men's barracks. The first floor of this large building is occupied by a sizable kitchen, a workshop, and the enlisted men's mess halls. The second floor is divided into two rooms which together housed about seventy men.

The large stone storehouse is found toward the western portion of the road. This building features several storerooms, two guard rooms, and a jail with four cells. There is a two-story building just to the north of the stone house which is a twentieth century building not in keeping with the rest of the fort's nineteenth century period structures.

In the northwest part of the fort is officers' quarters number two. It is quite similar to officers' quarters number one.

Fort Ontario is undergoing renovations and not all rooms in one of the officers' quarters are finished, although there are videos to show what they will look like.

Fort visitors can also see underground artillery casements (chambers), rifle galleries, and visit the ramparts with breathtaking views of Lake Ontario that are mostly unchanged since ancient times.

BRIEF HISTORY

GEOGRAPHY

A recurring theme, with regard to historic sites, is the overwhelming importance of geography in influencing when, where, and how events take place, and this factor is prominent in the history of Fort Ontario. Fort Ontario sits on a bluff overlooking the mouth of the Oswego River as it empties into Lake Ontario. It has been an important geographic location for many centuries. In ancient times the Oswego River was part of a Native American route from what is now New York City, up the Hudson River to the mouth of the Mohawk River, west on that river to near its origin, then along a six-mile portage (called the Oneida Carrying Place) to Wood Creek, then across Oneida Lake to the Oswego River and on to Lake Ontario. This route allowed early travelers to travel from points west to the Atlantic Ocean or from the Atlantic Ocean into the heart of North America. Of course traveling by water was by far the most important method of getting from one place to another well into the nineteenth century.

THE FUR TRADE AND EARLY FORTS IN THE AREA

Another factor determining much of the course of events after the arrival of Europeans in North America is the huge economic importance of the fur trade. Animal furs and especially beaver skins were in high demand in Europe for hat making and other clothing manufacture. Fur trade profits could be huge. The Indians supplied most of the furs by trading them to European fur traders in exchange for European goods. Then the traders had to get their newly obtained furs to Europe, especially via the ports of New York and Montreal. The water route from Oswego to New York provided a way to get furs to the New York market. Traders could also go from Oswego to Montreal by following the St. Lawrence River. Oswego was an excellent location for both trading partners to meet, and thus the English built a fur trading post at Oswego on the west side of the Oswego River in 1722. A log palisade was erected around the post for protection. Then in 1727 a stone blockhouse was added for further defensive strength. This was called Fort Burnet, and its low ground next to the west side of the river made for easy access by fur-laden canoes. Later Fort Burnet was again strengthened by a stone wall and called Fort Pepperell.

THE FIRST FORT ONTARIO

The first Fort Ontario was built on high ground across the Oswego River from Fort Pepperell. It was an eight-point star-shaped wooden stockade which could accommodate about three hundred soldiers. It was nearly eight hundred feet in circumference, fourteen feet high, and had a large moat around it. The fort was often referred to as the Fort of the Six Nations. It was defended by some light artillery, and though useful, it was not impregnable. In the mid-eighteenth century Fort Ontario (Fort of the Six Nations) was just part of the defenses of the important fur trading settlement of Oswego. Other defenses in the area were Fort Oswego (previously known as Fort Pepperell) and Fort George, both on the west side of the Oswego River. Also, significant earthworks had been built around the forts.

FRENCH AND INDIAN WAR AND THE
SECOND FORT ONTARIO

In August 1756 during the French and Indian War (1755–1763) the French General Marquis de Montcalm attacked Oswego. As a result, Fort Ontario was abandoned. During their occupation, the French destroyed Fort Ontario as well as the other defensive works in the area.

Later in the war, in 1759, the British built a new fort on the same site as the destroyed Fort Ontario. This time the British used the very latest European military technology to construct a large earthen and timber fortification that would seem to be very strong indeed. This second Fort Ontario featured barracks enough to accommodate about five hundred soldiers and was surrounded by a dry moat and extensive earthworks. Another strong feature of the fort was the use of redoubts (small square or rectangular mini-forts) scattered on high ground outside of the main fortification to provide a first line of defense. The French and Indian War ended formally in 1763 with France relinquishing her land claims in North America.

PONTIAC'S REBELLION

Following the British victory in the French and Indian War, the British changed their gift-giving policy with regard to Native Americans. The Indians valued the gift-giving process as an important diplomatic process which enhanced good relations between peoples. In 1763, the British leaders ended the policy of gift giving. This led to an Indian uprising known as Pontiac's Rebellion. Pontiac was a charismatic Ottawa leader who led the uprising. In 1766 with the rebellion rapidly losing momentum, Fort Ontario played host to a very important meeting between Pontiac and British superintendent of Indian Affairs Sir William Johnson. On July 25, 1766, the two men signed a treaty ending Pontiac's Rebellion.

THE AMERICAN REVOLUTION

The next involvement of Fort Ontario in our history occurred in 1777 during the American Revolutionary War. The British strategy that year involved a plan to cut off the northeast, especially Boston, from the rest of the colonies, defeat that section, and then attack the remaining American colonies which would have lost the will to fight by the capture of Boston. To carry out this plan three groups of British forces would converge at Albany. General John Burgoyne would invade the colonies from Canada through Lake Champlain to Lake George and down the Hudson River to Albany. General Howe would bring his forces up the Hudson River from New York to Albany. To protect these forces from American attacks from the west, General Barry St. Leger would bring his Loyalists and British Indians to Fort Ontario in Oswego and then travel east through the Mohawk Valley, capture the lightly held Fort Stanwix, and then proceed to the Albany area.

On July 22, 1777, General St. Leger and his forces landed at Fort Ontario to spend the night and get organized. St. Leger had nearly 1,600 men consisting of eight hundred Indians (led by Joseph Brant) along with about the same number of a mixed group of British Regulars and Canadian volunteers. The next day this army left Fort Ontario and headed southeast toward Fort Stanwix anticipating an easy capture of that fort. However, the Americans proved themselves to be much stronger than expected. After a prolonged and unsuccessful siege of Fort Stanwix and a fierce battle with the American Militia (led by the heroic General Herkimer) at Oriskany, St. Leger, who had been abandoned by his demoralized Indians, was forced to retreat back to Fort Ontario and subsequently back to Canada.

The British plan to separate New England from the rest of the colonies was a complete failure after General Burgoyne with his army was surrounded and forced to surrender in October 1777 at Saratoga. Shortly thereafter Fort Ontario was abandoned by the British. In July 1778 the Americans of the Third New York Regiment based at Fort Stanwix advanced to Oswego and completely destroyed the second Fort Ontario.

THE THIRD FORT ONTARIO

In 1782 four years after the second Fort Ontario had been destroyed by American forces, the British reoccupied Oswego and built the third Fort Ontario. In 1781 General George Washington had forced the surrender of the British main army at Yorktown, Virginia, effectively ending the Revolutionary War (although the peace treaty was not signed until 1783). Nevertheless the British maintained their presence at Fort Ontario, causing General Washington to order an attack on the fort in 1783. The attack led by Lieutenant Colonel Marinus Willett failed because of severe winter weather, and the stubborn British held on to the fort until 1796 when they finally turned it over to the United States.

WAR OF 1812

Life at Fort Ontario was relatively uneventful for more than fifteen years until the War of 1812 broke out between the United States and England. Toward the end of that conflict, in 1814, the fort was attacked by the British and destroyed. Subsequently the parcel of land on which Fort Ontario had been situated fell into a period of disuse and neglect, until tensions once again arose between the United States and Britain. This time the problem was boundary issues between Canada and the United States. Construction by the United States of the forth version of Fort Ontario was begun in 1839 and completed five years later.

FINAL VERSION AND LATER USES

This new version of the fort is essentially the fort that we see today. The new Fort Ontario featured an earth and timber construction with a sloping outer wall around the perimeter. Inside are the officers' and enlisted men's barracks, the powder magazine, and the storehouse. This version of the fort could accommodate 120 soldiers. Nothing ever came of the implied threat from Canada that had caused the new construction

During the Civil War more modifications were begun on Fort Ontario and included the addition of east and west guardhouses and replacement of the sloping outer walls with vertical stone masonry. In 1872 congress failed to provide money to continue the modifications at the fort, and it was essentially neglected for the rest of the nineteenth century. In 1901 Fort Ontario was temporarily abandoned.

In 1903 the fort was re-garrisoned and expanded with new construction. This new activity was short-lived however, and in 1905 the fort was again abandoned.

The year 1928 found Fort Ontario once again being extensively used by the army in various capacities including as an officers' club and housing for junior officers. By the beginning of World War II there were more than one hundred buildings in and around the fort.

During World War II the fort was used as a unique emergency refugee center for survivors of the Nazi holocaust.

In 1946 after the ownership of the fort was transferred to the state of New York to be used as housing for veterans and their families, and was used as such until 1953.

Fort Ontario became a state historic site in 1949 and a national historic landmark in 1970.

TODAY

Fort Ontario is currently being restored to its 1870 self. Guides and reenactors dressed in period clothing help visitors learn about the fort and envision its interesting past.

The mouth of the Oswego River has been important economically and militarily since before Europeans first began traveling to the interior of North America in the 1600s. Standing on the ramparts of Fort Ontario, a visitor can look at a wonderful example of a nineteenth century fort, and perhaps as we look out to the mouth of the Oswego River, we can almost see the French explorers, the English fur traders, and the Indians who used this strategic area in centuries past.

III.

Old Erie Canal

State Historic Park

Photo credit Wikipedia. Declared public domain.(Includes Erie
Canal Village and Chittenango Landing Canal Boat Museum)

Location: RD #2 Andrus Road. Kirkville, NY 13082 (address listed on Web site). The Old Erie Canal State Historic Park (OECSHP) is a thirty-six-mile-long stretch of the old Erie Canal. There are many access points, but the two best are; at the Chittenango Landing Canal Boat Museum in Chittenango (717 Lakeport Road), and at the east end of the park from the Erie Canal village, 5789 Rome New London Road (Routes 46 and 49), Rome.

Directions: To get to the Eastern terminus of the park (**at Erie Canal Village**). From the New York State Thruway heading east; take exit 33 Verona, then Rt. 365 towards Rome, then 49 West (Rome New London Road) to #5789. From the thruway heading west; take exit 31 and follow Rt. 49 west; or take exit 32 (Westmoreland), follow R233 north towards Rome; pick up 49 west to the village.

See below for directions to **Chittenango Landing Boat Museum**:

Coordinates: Erie Canal Village. 43.226190 N, -75.503203 W Chittenango Landing Canal Boat Museum. 43.059654 N, -75.870728

Season: The Park has many crossroad access points which are always open and free. The eastern terminus, Erie Canal Village, is open from late May to early September.

Admission: (To the Erie Canal village) Modest fee for adults. Senior and child discounts.

Contacts: Erie Canal Village. 5789 Rome New London Rd., Rome, New York 13440
Phone: (315)337-3999, (315)687-7821, as listed on Web Site.
Email: mandm20005@twcny.com
Web: http://www.eriecanalvillage.net/

DESCRIPTION

The Old Erie Canal State Historic Park (OECSHP) is a thirty-six-mile stretch of the original Erie Canal and the towpath that runs along next to it. "Original" needs to be clarified. The original Erie Canal was completed in 1825 and was four feet deep, deep enough for the boats of that era. Later, as boats grew larger, the canal was deepened to seven feet. This work was finished in 1862, and this is the original Erie Canal that the park preserves. However, traces of the original "original" canal (the four-feet-deep channel) can be seen at several places in the park.

The OECSHP runs from the town of DeWitt (just east of Syracuse) to the outskirts of the city of Rome, for a total of nearly thirty-six miles. The Canal Way Trail runs alongside of it. The park is advertised as a place for kayaking, canoeing, walking, biking, cross-country skiing, horseback riding, and snowmobiling. Please note that, although the park does advertise itself as a place for kayaking and canoeing, those opportunities tend to be few and far between. This is due to a lack of water in some sections, stagnant and smelly water in others, and obstructions too. It is difficult to clear bridges in a few places. Any navigable sections tend to be toward the DeWtt end of the park, and perhaps should be checked out before bringing along your canoe or kayak.

There are a number attractions and facilities along the length of the park. Just east of the western end of the park is Cedar Bay Picnic area which has parking, picnic tables, and bathrooms. Near Manlius Center there is a footbridge that leads to Green Lakes State Park. About one-third of the way, from west to east, is Pools Brook Picnic area with parking and bathrooms, located on a short road called Andrus Road off Pools Brook Road.

CHITTENANGO LANDING CANAL BOAT MUSEUM

About halfway through the park (just north of Chittenango) on the south side of the canal is Chittenango Landing Canal Boat Museum. Visitors wishing to broaden their Erie Canal experience should definitely include a visit to this interesting museum. One of the main features of the museum is an excavated three-bay dry dock (built in 1855) where craftsmen built and repaired the standard Erie Canal cargo boats. These boats measured ninety-eight feet long and were designed to carry grains, lumber, coal, and farm produce, to eastern markets.

Other interesting features of the museum include a sawmill, a blacksmith shop, a mule stable, a boarding house, and a sunken canal boat (visible when the water is reasonably clear. The museum explains and models the construction of the canal boats, and other aspects of Old Erie Canal life. Within a short walk is a reconstructed canal aqueduct.

Visitor information for the Canal Boat Museum:

Chittenango Landing Canal Boat Museum 717 Lakeport Road, Chittenango, NY 13037-9594
Contact: Phone: (315)687-3801
     Website: www.clcbm.org
     Email: info@clcbm.org
Season: May to June, Saturday and Sunday 1:00 pm – 4:00 pm
     July to August, Daily 11:00 pm – 3:00 pm
        September to October, Saturday and Sunday 1:00 pm – 4:00 pm
Admission: Modest fee, Under 12 free, Members free
Directions:

     From NYS thruway exit 34:
     Take route 13S to route 5, turn right at light, 6 miles to Chittenango. Turn right at light onto Lakeport Road. Museum is ½ mile on left.
     From NYS Thruway exit 34A:
     Take 481 (S) to exit 3E. Take route 5 east 10 miles to Chittenango. Go north on Lake port Road. Museum is ½ mile on left.

ERIE CANAL VILLAGE

Located at the eastern end of the OECSHP is the Erie Canal village, just west of the city of Rome. The Erie Canal Village features three museums, the Erie Canal Museum, the New York State Museum of Cheese, and the Harden Museum. The Erie Canal museum tells the story of the Erie Canal from inception in 1808 through the Barge Canal era in 1918. The Harden Museum contains an interesting collection of nineteenth century horse-drawn vehicles. The NYS Cheese Museum demonstrates the cheese-making process and its place in New York State history. In addition to the museums there are other interesting nineteenth century buildings including a black-smith shop, a settler's house, a barn, a store, Bennett's Tavern, a livery table, a schoolhouse, and a church meeting house. There is also a café (modern) and restrooms.

Visitor Information for the Erie Canal Village:

Address: 5789 Rome New London Road, routes 46, 49,
    Rome NY, 13440
Phone: (315)337-3999
Website: http://www.eriecanalvillage.net/.
Email: maudm20005@wcny.rr.com
Season: May 26 – September 1, Wed-Sat 10 am – 5:00 pm
Admissions: Modest fee. Child and Senior discounts, Train Ride sep-
    arate modest fee
Directions: see beginning of this chapter.

OTHER POINTS OF INTEREST

There are a number of interesting aqueducts (bridges that carry water) to view throughout the park, some of which are listed below:

1. Oneida Creek Aqueduct – located just west of the village of Durhamville, completed in 1856
2. Cowaselon Creek Aqueduct – located in the middle of the park on Canal Street east of the village of Canastota, also completed in 1856
3. Chittenango Creek Aqueduct – located one-half mile west of Chittenango Landing Canal Boat Museum; comprised

of three spans over Chittenango Creek and completed in 1856

4. Butternut Creek Aqueduct – located in the town of DeWitt

Note: In most of the aqueducts, the original wooden planking has been replaced with concrete.

1. Cooper's Tubular Arch Bridge

Hill Street Bridge is a tubular bridge built in 1886 and moved to the OECSHP in Dewitt in 1975. It now spans the original Erie Canal in the park, carrying pedestrians and service vehicles.

In summary, the Old Erie Canal State Historic Park contains many remnants and restorations of both stages (1825 and 1856) of the original Erie Canal, and several museums, all of which give visitors an exciting glimpse back into early New York State history. The park is not perfect in that there are some sections that have lapsed into partial disrepair. However, to learn about and see parts of this very important early development in the history of our country is a fascinating experience.

BRIEF HISTORY

(See also the introduction chapter in this book for a discussion of the economic impact of the Erie Canal on New York State.)

CONCEPTION AND IMPLEMENTATION

As previously noted the idea for the canal first came from merchants, especially grain merchants, who wanted to expand their markets. A canal from Buffalo, New York, to the Hudson River would create a connection between the Great Lakes and the eastern seaboard (because the mouth of the Hudson River empties into the Atlantic Ocean at New York). Also, shipping goods on a canal would be faster and cheaper than the horse-drawn carts then in use.

Besides the obvious expense, there were several other major obstacles to overcome in building the canal. There is a rise in elevation of six hundred feet between the eastern seaboard and Buffalo. This would require engineers to build a series of locks along the 363-mile length of the canal. Also, there were no steam shovels or other power equipment yet, so the canal would have to be built by manual labor. Because of these monumental obstacles, there were many detractors and disbelievers in the project. Fortunately, one of the believers in the project was New York governor DeWitt Clinton, and he was eventually able to get the New York State legislature to provide seven million dollars (a lot of money back then) to build the Erie Canal.

Work on "Clinton's Ditch" or "Clinton's folly," as the canal was sometimes referred to, began in 1817 in Rome. The "ditch" was forty feet wide and four feet deep, and as the digging was all done by hand, progress was slow. The bottom of the canal was lined with clay, while the sides were lined with stone and inlaid with clay. The excavated dirt was used to create a walkway, or towpath, alongside the canal.

Finally in 1825 the canal was finished and open for business. To celebrate, Governor Clinton took a canal boat from Buffalo to New York City. It took him eight days to complete that journey.

GROWTH

Business on the canal grew rapidly. Soon, in an effort to increase efficiency, canal boats began to get bigger. The larger early boats ran up to ninety-six feet, but even larger boats would be much more efficient. To accommodate larger boats, a project was launched, in the late 1850s, to enlarge the canal. The expansion of the canal was completed by 1862, and the new dimensions of the canal were seventy feet wide at the surface, down to fifty-two feet wide at the bottom, and seven feet deep. Now boats up to 110 feet long and sixteen feet wide could be launched, significantly increasing the per boat carrying capacity. The new channel was sometimes built right over the original and sometimes beside it.

The same enlargement process occurred again in the early twentieth century, and by 1918 the canal had been enlarged several times. The new canal was now called the Barge Canal and retains that name to the present. By the 1940s trucks, trains, and planes had completely replaced canal transportation and made the Barge Canal obsolete for commercial purposes. Today it is used only for recreation.

Please note that in some places in New York State sections of the Barge Canal are referred to as the Erie Canal for unknown reasons.

Statewide there are quite a few remnants of the real Original Erie Canal, especially in the imperfect, but wonderful, Old Erie Canal State Historic Park. Here visitors can view some of the original Erie Canal "ditch" and perhaps visualize grain-laden barges being pulled by mules through the nineteenth century New York State countryside.

IV.

Fort Stanwix

National Monument

Interior of Fort Stanwix. Photo by the author.

Location: 112 East Park St., Rome, NY 13440

Directions: From the West: take NYS thruway to exit 33, follow 365 E. Turn left onto Routes 26, 49, 69 to Rome (Erie Blvd E). Turn right onto N James St. in Rome.

From the East: Take NYS thruway to exit 32. Take Rte 233 north to 365 west. Take 365 W to Rtes 26, 49, 69 (Erie Blvd E) to Rome. Turn right onto N James St.

Parking is available in the Municipal Parking lot across James St. from the Fort.

Coordinates: 43.211974 N, -75.454745 W

Season: Main season. The National Park Service Visitor Center (Willett Center) adjacent to the fort is open daily from April 1 through October 31. Hours are from 9:00 am to 5:00 pm During that period the fort itself is open from 9:15 am until 4:45 pm. Also, during this period there are several scheduled fort tours conducted by park rangers each day.

Note. The Willett Center is open nearly all year though the fort itself is not open for unlimited visitation outside the main season, except for daily scheduled guided tours of the fort. The exact schedule is rather complex, and it is recommended that you check the Web site (or call [315]338-7730) if you want to visit on dates outside of the main season so that you can be sure to arrive around the time of a scheduled fort tour. There is a period from mid-January to late March when the Willett Center (and fort) is closed on Monday and Tuesday of each week. Again, check the Web site or call the number to be sure the site is open when you wish to visit. It is a visit you will not forget.

Admission: There is no admission fee.

Contacts:

Web: http://www.nps.gov/fost/index.htm.

Phone: (315)338-7730.

DESCRIPTION

Fort Stanwix National Monument is a very important historic site featuring an eighteenth century fort reconstructed on its original location and administered by the National Park Service. The site is located in the city of Rome, New York, and consists of the fort itself, and an extensive visitor's center, called the Willett Center, all in a parklike setting.

The current fort is a faithful reconstruction of the original fort. Original plans and materials were used to ensure that the fort's appearance is exactly as it was during the American Revolutionary War. The original fort was built in 1758 by British Brigadier General John Stanwix as an important post in the French and Indian War. The fort was neglected after that war was won by the British in 1763. In 1776 General George Washington ordered the fort to be rebuilt in order to protect the western frontier. At that time the name was changed to Fort Schuyler.

The visitors' center, named the Willett Center, consists of a site orientation facility, a museum with a number of interesting artifacts and a gift shop. Helpful National Park Service rangers are on hand to orient the visitor and get them started on their tour of the adjacent fort.

Fort Stanwix itself is a low multilevel wooden four-sided structure surrounded by a wooden palisade. There is a projecting pointed Bastion (to allow defenders to fire their muskets parallel to the walls) at each corner of the fort and a sizable ditch on the north side inside the palisade. The center of the fort is an open rectangular parade ground. Running along almost the entire west side of the parade ground is a common soldiers' barracks (now containing exhibits). A nearly identical structure runs along the east wall and was also used as a barracks. Along the north side are six low individual rooms called the north casement, also used for common soldiers' barracks, although the Americans used the area for officers' quarters. Behind the east and west barracks are the east and west casements, more barracks. Through the east wall of the fort is a sally port, used by soldiers to slip out of the fort and get water from a nearby stream. During the siege of the fort (in 1777), Colonel Willett used the sally port to escape the fort and run for help from American Militia forces east of Fort Stanwix at Fort Dayton.

Three walking trails surround the fort and give visitors an excellent view of its exterior. There is parking in the municipal ramp garage across James Street from the fort. It is suggested that visitors start at the Willett Center.

Fort Stanwix National Monument is very well maintained by the National Park Service and your visit is greatly enhanced by the well-informed and friendly rangers. The site is extremely interesting, especially when you know about the important history-changing events that occurred there in the eighteenth century (see below).

BRIEF HISTORY

THE BEGINNING

Fort Stanwix began life as an important English post constructed along the "Oneida Carrying Place" portage during the French and Indian War. As we have seen, water routes were all-important in colonial times. Travelling by boat (or canoe) was simply the easiest and sometimes only way to get from here to there. A critical route for travelling from the New York City area to western New York and beyond was to take the Hudson River to the Mohawk River, travel up that river to a six-mile portage called the Oneida Carrying Place, then back into the water using Wood Creek to get to Oneida Lake, then on to Oswego on the shore of Lake Ontario. This route was used for thousands of years by Native Americans, and later by European traders as well. Fort Stanwix was erected along the Oneida Carrying Place to be able to control this route to and from central New York.

The fort was built in 1758 during the French and Indian War by British Brigadier General John Stanwix. Its purpose was to stop the French and their Indians allies from using the before mentioned route to attack the Mohawk Valley and other central New York settlements. The plan worked, and the French invasion ended. The fort also provided a staging area for other English operations during that war. After the English won the war, officially in 1763, the fort was abandoned and fell into disrepair.

AFTER THE FRENCH AND INDIAN WAR

The period following the British victory in the French and Indian War featured much conflict over land ownership between Native American groups and westward moving English settlers and traders. The British government seemed sincere in wanting to work out an arrangement with the Indians for a peaceful coexistence. Mohawk Valley trader and wealthy estate owner Sir William Johnson was very influential with the Iroquois Confederacy, especially the Mohawks, and had had many successful negotiations with them. He was the right man to deal with Indian issues and was appointed by the British to the post of superintendent of Indian Affairs. In October 1768 Johnson hosted a very important treaty negotiation with the Indians at the abandoned Fort Stanwix. Thousands of Indians came to participate in the talks. As a result of the negotiations a treaty (referred to as the Boundary Line Treaty) was signed in early November in which the Iroquois agreed to cede lands east and south of the Ohio River to the English. In return the Indians received more than $50,000 worth of gifts. After this conference Fort Stanwix was nearly forgotten and for years was manned by only a few soldiers. In 1774 the fort was abandoned by the British and fell into disrepair until called upon to serve the most important role in its history.

THE AMERICAN REVOLUTION

The American Revolution began at Lexington and Concord in 1775. In 1776 the Continental Congress ordered General George Washington to have Fort Stanwix rebuilt in order to preserve and protect the emerging nation's northwest frontier. The newly renovated fort was renamed Fort Schuyler in honor of Major General Phillip Schuyler (although many people continued to refer to it as Fort Stanwix as we do today).

BRITISH STRATEGY

The overall British strategy at this stage of the Revolutionary War was to separate the most ardent rebels, those in New England, from the rest of the country. Then by defeating New England the British hoped the rest of the country would easily fall. To accomplish this goal they planned to have General Howe and his army proceed north along the Hudson River from New York City and join up with General Burgoyne's army which was descending from Canada through the Lake Champlain, Lake George, and Hudson River corridor. These two armies would meet somewhere in the vicinity of Albany. Once accomplished this would effectively isolate New England from American forces to the south.

Part of the British Plan was to order Lieutenant Colonel (brevetted Brigadier General) Barry St. Leger to take his army to Oswego, New York, and then head southeast to capture the Americans' Fort Stanwix. After securing the fort St. Leger would proceed east to the Albany area and join up with the other two British armies. This would prevent American forces in central New York from joining up with the American forces, under General Horatio Gates, who had been dispatched to try to stall Burgoyne's march south along the Hudson River. Also, the British believed that if they captured Fort Stanwix it would be easier to get the Iroquois to more fully support them against the Americans. The British believed that Fort Stanwix was manned with a very small number of soldiers and that it would be easy to overwhelm them. The British could not have been more wrong in that assessment.

REBUILT

Following General Washington's orders, reconstruction work on the "new" Fort Stanwix was begun in June 1776 by Colonel Elias Dayton and his Third New Jersey Regiment of Continental soldiers. Colonel Peter Gansevoort, who commanded the Third New York Continental Regiment, relieved Colonel Dayton in April of 1777. Colonel Gansevoort's second in command was an enterprising, and brave, officer named Lieutenant Marinus Willett. With the re-garrisoning of the fort there were now nearly eight hundred continental soldiers in the fort. These were the men who would attempt to withstand a siege by the advancing British under Barry St. Leger.

SIEGE

As St. Leger neared Fort Stanwix, his Indian scouts reported that a column of American soldiers was in route to bolster the fort's defenses. St. Leger sent a "flying column" of about thirty of his regulars along with two hundred Iroquois to try to intercept the relief force, but they were too late. The relief column entered Fort Stanwix, with men and supplies, on August 2, just as the English "flying" column arrived. The British did manage to kill one man, capture another, and wound two more, but the fort was significantly strengthened. The next day, August 3, St. Leger arrived with the rest of his men.

St. Leger had a sizable force consisting of British regulars, American Loyalists, rangers, one hundred or so laborers, and about eight hundred Indians (mostly Seneca and Mohawks) led by Joseph Brant. St Leger's total force of about 1,600 men had seemed more than enough to capture what he had originally thought was a dilapidated fort with about sixty defenders. The strengthened fort with its much larger number of American defenders was an unexpected and unwelcome surprise for St. Leger.

The first step in St. Leger's plan was to try to intimidate the fort's defenders into giving up. To this end he paraded his entire force around the fort. All this accomplished was to make the defenders strengthen their resolve to prevent the British from proceeding into the Mohawk Valley. When his intimidation tactic failed, St. Leger sent a truce flag, to Gansevoort, bearing a proclamation from General Burgoyne. Gansevoort refused to respond, so St. Leger began siege operations. Artillery was placed on a low hill north of the fort, as Indians and Loyalists were encamped to the south and along the Mohawk River. On August 5 St. Leger received word that an American relief column was on its way up the Mohawk Valley towards the fort.

AMERICAN RELIEF FORCE AMBUSHED

The American relief force consisted of eight hundred men from the Tryon County Militia, led by General Nicholas Herkimer. They were coming from Fort Dayton, and by August 6 they were within ten miles of Fort Stanwix. St. Leger's reaction to the approach of the relief force was to pull the majority of his forces out of the siege lines, along with most of his Indians (led by Brant), and send them to ambush General Herkimer. The two forces collided on August 6 about six miles from Fort Stanwix, and a desperate battle ensued just outside the Oneida village of Oriska. American Casualties were numerous, including General Herkimer who was shot in the leg. By late in the day casualties were heavy on both sides, and many of Brandt's Indians had been killed by the Americans. This greatly demoralized Brant and his surviving followers, and they began to retreat back to the British lines at Fort Stanwix. At the end of the day, the Americans too had to withdraw, but so did all the British forces. This fight is called the Battle of Oriskany (for details on this epic battle see the chapter on the Oriskany Battlefield State Historic Site).

DEVASTATING AMERICAN SORTIE FROM THE FORT

While the Battle of Oriskany was going on, Lieutenant Colonel Willett led a force of 250 men out of Fort Stanwix and began to attack the nearby British camps. This type of maneuver had been requested by General Herkimer in a message sent to the fort several days previously. As Willett's men attacked, the greatly reduced British forces around the fort (the majority of them being at Oriskany) abandoned their positions. Willett's men proceeded to destroy the British camps, especially the Indians' camp, and confiscate a large amount of British supplies.

THE SIEGE CONTINUES BUT NOT FOR LONG

Despite their heavy losses at the Battle of Oriskany, the British had turned back General Herkimer's relief column. Now St. Leger again demanded that the fort surrender. The Americans would not consider surrender. St. Leger renewed his siege attacks, his lines moving ever closer to the fort. On August 8 Colonel Willett and a Lieutenant Stockwell slipped out of the fort and headed east to Fort Dayton in order to request more help. Willett ended up going all the way to Albany where General Phillip Schuyler approved a plan wherein General Benedict Arnold volunteered to lead a relief force of nine hundred men back to Fort Stanwix. Arnold also created some false intelligence to the effect that his force consisted of over three thousand men. This disturbing information reached St. Leger and his Indians. The already demoralized Indians proceeded to riot, steal liquor and other items, and flee to the forest. St. Leger was left with no alternative but to withdraw with his men back to Canada with what few supplies they could carry with them. They abandoned their tents, ammunition, and even their artillery. General Arnold arrived at the fort on August 23 to great cheers and salutes from the fort's new cannons.

EFFECTS OF THE FAILED SIEGE AND LATER HISTORY OF THE FORT

The failure of St. Leger to take Fort Stanwix and thus be able to support General Burgoyne along the Hudson River was a contributing factor to the British defeat at the Battles of Saratoga. The American victory at Saratoga was an important turning point in the revolutionary war. Another result of the failed British siege of Fort Stanwix was that the important Mohawk Valley was now under control of the Americans.

In 1779 the Fort Stanwix served as a staging area for an American raid on an Onondaga Indian village which had been supporting the British cause.

In 1781 the Americans abandoned Fort Stanwix because it had been partially destroyed by flooding and a fire.

In 1784, one year after the end of the Revolutionary War, the Treaty of Fort Stanwix was signed at Fort Stanwix by the United States and the Iroquois Six Nation Confederacy. This signaled the end of hostilities between the two groups. The fort continued to be used for many years as the site where the Iroquois would come on June 1 to receive payments for land they had ceded to New York State. After 1815 the fort fell into disrepair and parts of it were built over by the City of Rome in the 1830s. In the 1970s the City of Rome partnered with the National Park Service to build a faithful replica of the fort using the original plans and documents.

Visiting Fort Stanwix National Monument, in Rome, New York, is a memorable experience. It is easy to visualize the siege operations, the British rush to Oriskany to stop General Herkimer's relief forces, and those feisty and brave Americans who defended the fort and would not give in to St. Leger's attacks.

V.

Oriskany Battlefield

State Historic Site

The hillside where General Herkimer's men rallied. The ravine where the British sprung their ambush is visible in the background. (Photo by the author)

Location: 7801 State Route 69, Box 275, RD1, Oriskany, NY 13424

Directions: From NYS Thruway take exit 32, than take Rte 233 to Rte 69 (The site is two miles west of Oriskany Village.)

GPS Coordinates: 43.177259 N, -75.369521 W

Season: Gates open April through October 10:00 am to 4:00 pm. Lawn and trails open all year

Admission: Free

Contact: C/O Fort Stanwix National Monument. 112 E. Park St. Rome, NY 13440
Phone: (315)338-7730 or (315)768-7224
Web: http://www.nysparks.com/historic-sites/21/details.aspx

DESCRIPTION

At first glance the Oriskany Battlefield State Historic Site, located in Upstate New York, is not much to look at, just some pleasant parkland. However if visitors have familiarized themselves with what occurred there, it can be an absolutely thrilling place to visit. The intense battle that took place there was one of the bloodiest of the American Revolution. Its results contributed significantly to an American victory in two of the most important battles in the history of the world, the Battles of Saratoga.

As you enter the site, driving down a small entrance road to the parking lot, you will notice the large spire-like memorial (obelisk) toward the left side of the field. The rest of the field is mostly open and grass covered (at the time of the battle it was heavily forested). As you reach the back of the site, you will find a steep sloped and fairly deep ravine which contains quite a number of beech and oak trees. A small creek (Battle Brook) still flows through the ravine, and the bottomland along the creek is quite swampy. There is a small visitors' center located in the northwest corner of the site. Scattered along the edge of the ravine are placards describing what occurred at that particular location. There is a stone marker designating the approximate location of the Beech tree under which the mortally wounded General Nicholas Herkimer sat smoking his pipe while directing and encouraging his troops.

(Note that it is not necessary for the visitor's center to be open in order to enjoy this extremely historic place, nor is it necessary to combine a visit here with a visit to nearby Fort Stanwix National Historic Monument, although the two are closely interrelated and a visit to both sites would be ideal.)

BRIEF HISTORY

The Battle of Oriskany, fought during the Revolutionary War on August 6, 1777, was a relatively small, but extremely fierce and bloody affair. The battle was fought in and around a ravine six miles east of the Patriot's Fort Stanwix. On one side was a force of eight hundred Patriot militiamen (Americans wanting independence from the British Crown) of the Tryon County Militia along with about sixty Oneida Indian allies. These Patriot militiamen were advancing to relieve the British siege of Fort Stanwix. Their opponents were a combined force of British Loyalists (Colonists who were loyal to the British Crown) along with British allied Indians, totaling more than 450 men. The British forces were sent to intercept the Patriots before they could reach Fort Stanwix.

Though militarily it could not be considered a victory for the Americans, the overall effect of the Battle of Oriskany and the subsequent failed siege of Fort Stanwix contributed significantly to the monumental defeat of the British regular army at Saratoga in the following weeks. The battles of Saratoga were two battles between British and American forces (fought on September 19, 1777, and October 7, 1777) which resulted in British General John Burgoyne's surrender of all his forces to the Americans on October 17, 1777. This is considered the turning point of the Revolutionary War.

BRITISH STRATEGY

As most American schoolchildren know, the actual fighting of the American War for Independence (the Revolutionary War) started on April 19, 1775, at Lexington and Concord, just outside of Boston. By 1777 the war was focused mainly in the northern colonies and no clear victor had yet emerged. The British strategy to defeat the American "rebels" in 1777 was to invade the newly independent colonies from Canada by advancing down the Lake Champlain, Lake George, and Hudson River corridor to Albany where that army would meet up with other British forces moving north from New York City. These movements would be supported by a third British army coming east from Oswego along the Mohawk Valley. The three armies would converge near Albany, New York. The effect of these actions would be to isolate New England (especially Boston), considered to be the hotbed of rebellion, from the rest of the colonies. The British believed that once New England was conquered the remaining colonies would quickly capitulate.

Commanding the British invasion from Canada was General John "Gentleman Johnny" Burgoyne. Burgoyne with his 7,200 British and German regulars would proceed south across Lake Champlain to Fort Crown Point, then continue ten more miles to Fort Ticonderoga, then along Lake George to the Hudson River road, and on to Albany. At Albany Burgoyne would hook up with British forces arriving from the south under General William Howe, and the British force from the Mohawk Valley to the west led by Colonel (brevetted General) Barry St. Leger.

If the British had successfully accomplished their plan, they would indeed have isolated the rebellious colonies into two sections, which could possibly have been conquered separately. That result did not happen, as we know. In fact this campaign was a world-history-changing disaster for the British ending with a stunning American victory at the battles of Saratoga. The Battle of Oriskany, though neither a victory nor a defeat for the Americans, played an important role in the American's great success at Saratoga.

ST. LEGER ADVANCES

The British plan called for General Barry St. Leger to take his army to Oswego, follow the Oswego River to Lake Oneida, and then follow Wood Creek to the "Oneida carrying place" portage. From there St. Leger would follow the Mohawk River to its mouth at the Hudson

River near Albany and unite with Generals Burgoyne and Howe. Part of this plan required that St. Leger capture the American Fort guarding the six-mile portage between Wood Creek and the Mohawk River. That fort was Fort Stanwix, which the British believed they could capture with little difficulty. They were very wrong.

General St. Leger began his expedition from La Chine, Canada, on June 23, 1777. He first headed for Oswego where he arrived on July 14, 1777. From there he planned to proceed on to Fort Stanwix, which he still imagined he would easily capture. St. Leger's army consisted of British Regular soldiers, some surprisingly light artillery, eighty Germans mercenaries, 350 Loyalists led by Sir John Johnson, a company of Butlers Rangers, and 100 Canadian Laborers, for a total of about 750 men. Originally the British thought that this force would be strong enough to easily take Fort Stanwix (St. Leger had originally been told there were only sixty Patriot soldiers garrisoning the fort). However, intelligence received from some Patriot deserters and Indian scouts informed St. Leger that the fort had recently been considerably strengthened. St. Leger's scouts told him that the fort was now defended by about six hundred Regular soldiers and that the Americans knew that St. Leger was coming. (Oneida scouts loyal to the Americans had informed the Americans of St. Legers plan to capture the fort.) To adjust to this new situation, St. Leger, while at Oswego, added a large force of British friendly Indians, mostly Mohawks and Seneca of the Iroquois Confederacy, commanded by the Mohawk Chief Joseph Brant. This combined force of over 1,500 (some estimates say as many as 1,700) men now rapidly headed east toward Fort Stanwix.

FORT STANWIX

Fort Stanwix (sometimes called Fort Schuyler) was originally built by the British in 1758 during the French and Indian War. As with many forts of the period, its location was on a strategically critical water route. In this case the water route ran from the Hudson River along the aforementioned path that eventually ended at Oswego on Lake Ontario. The fort was built to control the "Oneida carrying place," which was the six-mile portage between Wood Creek and the Mohawk River. After the French and Indian War ended (officially in 1763), the fort was abandoned and fell into disrepair. When the Revolutionary War began, the fort was occupied by the Americans and refurbished. In 1777 as General St. Leger approached Fort Stanwix, the Patriot forces garrisoning the fort numbered 750 Continental Regulars (the Third New York Regiment and the Ninth Massachusetts Regiment) commanded by Lieutenant Colonel Peter Gansevoort.

St. Leger and his forces arrived in front of Fort Stanwix on August 2, 1777, and immediately began their siege.

GENERAL HERKIMER'S RELIEF FORCE

In the meantime, word (through Oneida Indian Scouts) of St. Leger's attack on Fort Stanwix had reached interested Patriot parties including General Nicholas Herkimer in nearby Tryon County. As a response to this crisis, a relief force made up of Tryon County Militia was formed at Fort Dayton, thirty miles southeast of Fort Stanwix. This force was commanded by General Herkimer. Herkimer's army consisted of eight hundred volunteer militia (mostly poorly trained German farmers), and sixty Oneida Indians (most of the Iroquois Confederacy had sided with the British in this war but a group of the Oneidas were fighting for the Patriot cause). General Herkimer and his men began marching toward Fort Stanwix on August 4, and August 5 found them camped just outside the small Oneida town of Oriska. Here the general sent three advance runners to alert Colonel Gansevoort, at Fort Stanwix, that the relief force was on its way. The runners were also to tell Gansevoort to coordinate Herkimer's attack on the British with a sortie from the fort against the British camps located near the fort. Gansevoort was to signal Herkimer with three cannon shots when he began his sortie and then Herkimer would begin his attack.

AMBUSH

Unfortunately for the Americans, St. Leger learned of General Herkimer's advancing militia. Molly Brant, Joseph's sister and also a Loyalist, informed Brant of Herkimer's relief force. To counter this threat St. Leger dispatched a sizable force to intercept the Americans before they could reach the fort. This force consisted of a detachment of Loyalists along with many of the British allied Native Americans, nearly four hundred warriors. This British detachment was led by Loyalist Sir John Johnson and Joseph Brant. Their plan was to set up an ambush along the road that they knew General Herkimer must take to get to the fort. As the sun was coming up on the morning of August 6, the British ambushers were in their places along the road, about six miles east of Fort Stanwix.

The spot chosen for the ambush was where the road passed through a ravine. There was (still is) a small stream passing through the ravine, and the slopes of the ravine were heavily wooded. The British and their Indian allies concealed themselves in a semicircle on the west side of the ravine, leaving the eastern approach open for the Americans to walk into the trap. Once General Herkimer and all his men were in the trap, the east end would be sealed and the Americans would be surrounded.

General Herkimer had originally wanted to wait in his camp until he heard Colonel Gansevoort's signal that he had begun his sortie from Fort Stanwix. This plan did not sit well with some of Herkimer's officers who accused him of cowardice. Apparently this bothered the general and thus early on August 6 the militia began heading down the road toward Fort Stanwix.

PREMATURELY SPRUNG

A sometimes fatal flaw of Native American warriors was impatience, and that trait demonstrated itself in this ambush. About 10:00 am General Herkimer and some of his men (about six hundred) had passed through the ravine and were ascending the high ground to the west of it when the impatient British Indians prematurely opened fire. The problem for the British was that a significant number of Herkimer's men (two hundred, his rear guard) had not yet entered the trap. The result was that these men escaped the encirclement and headed back to the east from whence they had come, with quite a number of the British Indians in hot pursuit.

AN INTENSE FIGHT

Meanwhile General Herkimer and the remainder of his men were the objects of a blistering musket fire from three sides delivered by the Loyalists and their remaining Indians. General Herkimer himself had been among the first casualties when a musket ball shattered his leg and killed his horse. Although his men wanted him to retire from the fight, the general would have none of it. Instead he had some of his men prop him up under a beech tree where he continued to direct his soldiers and smoke his pipe. The intense fire fight had been going on for about forty-five minutes (some sources say more than an hour) when a sudden rainstorm forced a halt to the proceedings.

Thus far the Patriot militia had been taking a lot of casualties, many of which were caused by Indians swooping in on the men and attacking them with battle-axes while they were reloading their muskets. To counter this action General Herkimer took advantage of the rain delay to order his men to pair up and to be sure that one of the men was loaded and ready to fire at attackers while the second man reloaded.

THE BATTLE RESUMES

After about an hour the rain stopped, the sky cleared and the battle began anew. General Herkimer and all of his men were now on the west side of the ravine, and the attack continued to be fearsome. However, now the British allied Indians were beginning to be seriously affected by their severe losses. They had lost a number of chiefs and were rapidly losing interest in continuing the battle. At this point a second detachment of Loyalists arrived and pretended to be Americans by turning their coats inside out. However, this ruse was quickly discovered, and these men were fiercely attacked at close quarters by the Patriots.

THE BRITISH WITHDRAW

With Herkimer's militia putting up a ferocious resistance, knowledge that their base camp had been destroyed by a sortie from Fort Stanwix, with no victory in sight, and with their many losses, the British-allied Indians began to withdraw back to the British camps near Fort Stanwix. Their Loyalist allies, limited in numbers from the beginning, had no choice but to withdraw with their Indian allies. The Patriots were now in control of the battlefield, and the Battle of Oriskany was over.

Though militarily this battle would not be considered a victory for the Patriots, it was not a defeat either. American losses were in the range of 150 to 200 killed, including General Herkimer who died on August 16 after having his leg amputated. British losses were one hundred to two hundred killed (reports vary), many, if not most, of them Indians.

BACK AT THE FORT

While the Battle of Oriskany was being fought in and around the ravine six miles east of Fort Stanwix, action was also occurring back at the fort. The fort's garrison, led by Lieutenant Colonel Marinus Willett, made a large (about 250 men) sortie to the British and Indian camps outside the fort. Some Indians and Loyalists were killed, a great amount of various supplies were carried back to the fort, and much of what was left of the camps was destroyed. This caused great distress to the returning Loyalists and even more to their beleaguered Indian allies. The Indians had gone into battle nearly naked, and with the Americans confiscating so much of the camp's materials many of the Indians now had no clothing. A large number of the Indians became belligerent, stole British supplies, and proceeded to go home, deserting St. Leger.

ANOTHER AMERICAN RELIEF FORCE
AND A BRITISH FAILURE

After the Battle of Oriskany, the Tryon County Militia limped back to Fort Dayton led by Colonel Samuel Campbell. Meanwhile, General St. Leger continued on with his siege of Fort Stanwix though with little enthusiasm and far fewer Indian allies. Soon after the battered Patriots arrived back at Fort Dayton, General Phillip Schuyler organized another relief force. This time the militia would be led by Major General Benedict Arnold. As General Arnold was working his way toward Fort Stanwix, he cleverly led the British to think that he had more men (three thousand) than he actually did have (about eight hundred). The pending arrival of Arnold's men and the fact that many of his Indians had deserted him, led General St. Leger to lift the siege of Fort Stanwix on August 21 and head back to Canada. His mission was a complete failure.

AFTERMATH

The Battle of Oriskany was very important to the Patriot cause in the Revolutionary War. St. Leger's failure to capture Fort Stanwix, and hence his inability to move on to support General Burgoyne along the Hudson River, contributed significantly to the American victory at the Battles of Saratoga. Running low on supplies and abandoned to his fate by St. Leger as well as by the British forces which failed to appear from the south, General Burgoyne was forced to surrender his forces to the Americans on October 17, 1777. This undoubtedly was the turning point of the Revolutionary War. The Patriots had proved themselves to be tough, stubborn, and very capable.

With such profound effects on the history of the United States, it is perhaps a bit surprising that the Battle of Oriskany is not more well known than it is. Thankfully New York State has preserved this "hallowed ground" (administered by the National Park Service) so that we can visit the ravine and the hillside where General Herkimer and the Tryon County Militia fought their hearts out for the Patriot cause.

The site was declared a National Historic Landmark in 1962.

VI.

Johnson Hall

State Historic Site

Photo from US Government survey of historic buildings, 1936

Location: 139 Hall Avenue, Johnstown, NY 12095

Directions: Johnson Hall is less than a mile northwest of Johnstown, NY. From Thruway Exit 28 (Fonda-Fultonville), turn left on Riverside Drive, right across the Mohawk River into Fonda, left on Rte. 5, right on Route 30A (North) to Johnstown, left on E. Main (Rte 29 West) and follow Route 29 West with a right on N. William Street which curves left and becomes State Street. Follow State Street through one light to a second light and bear right on Hall Avenue. Hall Avenue dead ends in Johnson Hall's parking lot

Coordinates: 43.015284 N, -74.382472 W

Season: May through October – open Memorial Day, July Fourth, Labor Day

Admission: Small fee charged.

Contact: Phone (518)762-8712 or (518)762-2330

Web: http://www.nysparks.com/historic-sites/10/details.aspx.

Email for Friends of Johnson Hall:

friendsofjohnsonhall@gmail.bon.

Email for State Historic Site: Darlene.rogers@oprhp.ny.us

DESCRIPTION

Johnson Hall is an important National Historic Landmark located just outside of Johnstown that preserves the eighteenth century estate of Sir William Johnson along with eighteen acres of his land. Johnson was a very prominent and influential colonial leader in eighteenth century New York. He came to America from Ireland in 1738 to manage his uncle's lands near Amsterdam, New York. Johnson was ambitious and entrepreneurial and soon entered the fur trade as well as dabbling in land speculation. Demonstrating a remarkable rapport with the Indians from whom he obtained his furs (and land), Johnson was able to flourish in those businesses. Figures vary but some sources indicate Johnson may have owned more than four hundred thousand acres of the Mohawk Valley at one time.

In 1743 Johnson was able to buy land in the Mohawk River Valley upon which he erected his first home. His continuing success in the fur trade and other side businesses enabled him to amass a fortune. This allowed Johnson, in 1763, to build a third residence. This one would be truly suitable for a man with his wealth and influence. It would be called Johnson Hall (in the eighteenth century, "hall" meant the manor house of an estate with tenants), and included his residence as well as a sizable number of various supporting buildings and structures. There is a creek flowing through the property which allowed the construction of a sawmill and later a gristmill.

The main house at Johnson Hall is a large two-and-a-half-story Georgian-style home built of wood sitting on top of a rubble (stones) foundation. The wood siding was "rusticated" to make it look like stone blocks. The rectangular building has a hipped roof and is five bays wide and two deep.

There are two two-story buildings to the rear of the house (the three buildings form a courtyard). Both are constructed of stone rubble, and their second-story walls project a small amount over the first-story walls. Also, both buildings feature vertical openings at the eaves level just below a hipped roof. The building on the north side of the house is original and has two twelve-inch-by-twelve-inch windows. Also, there are two wooden doors, one on ground level and one on the second floor. The roof is made from wooden shingles. The first floor interior is carpeted, has plaster walls and ceiling, and is used as exhibit space.

The second two-story adjunct building (to the west) is a reconstruction of the original and was built in the late 1960s. The original was burned in 1866.

These two stone buildings (the original one and the one that burned in 1866) were built in the mid-eighteenth century. The function that Johnson envisioned for these two buildings is uncertain. Surviving documents suggest that they were used for storage, a study for Sir William, and slave quarters. Although strong, it doesn't seem that they were used for defensive purposes.

The setting of Johnson Hall is parklike with grassy areas as well as many trees scattered throughout. In some areas there are several picnic tables, and there is a stone overlook with a view of Johnson Hall and some of the surrounding area. Also, there is a statue of Sir

William Johnson on the southern tip of the property. It was constructed of stone in 1904 and is twelve feet tall. It pictures Johnson facing downhill toward his town, Johnstown, New York.

Sir William's property was far more than just a place for him to live; it was a thriving self-contained multi-functional community designed to demonstrate the benefits of living in the area to potential settlers. It was also where Johnson conducted his important fur trade business.

ARCHEOLOGICAL FINDINGS

Historic and ongoing archeological excavations, especially north and east of the house, have revealed how varied and extensive the various buildings and other constructions were at Johnson Hall. Some of the findings indicate the presence of a tunnel between the house and the west stone building and a likely blacksmith shop about 250 feet northwest of the house near the creek that runs through the property. Also found were remnants of a stockade between the two stone buildings, a possible blockhouse underneath the remnants of the Indian store (to the west of the main house), a concrete fountain pool and other unidentified buildings.

More recent archeological findings include the presence of another stockade and courtyard to the rear of the house, a rectangular cobblestone building in front of the house and another outbuilding to the southwest.

There is still much archeological work to be done on the property including an area that appears to be the site of the saw and grist mill which were powered by a raceway. In addition, there are documentary references that indicate the presence of a coach house, a shay house, a tailor shop, several barns, other dwellings, a gun shop, slave quarters, and a Lime Kiln. As archeologists get a more complete picture of Johnson's thriving manor, the result will undoubtedly add to our current picture of the site.

Over the years various modifications of the hall itself have taken place, especially during the nineteenth century. Thankfully efforts during the twentieth century have returned Johnson Hall to its original vintage eighteenth century architecture and furnishings.

BRIEF HISTORY

William Johnson was born in Ireland in 1715. He came to America in 1738 to manage his uncle's landholdings near Amsterdam, New York. Johnson apparently had a great entrepreneurial spirit, which he demonstrated quickly when he purchased a tract of land barely a year after arriving in America. Here he built the first of three homes he would eventually own. He would call this home Mount Johnson. It should be noted that Johnson moved in to this home with a woman named Catherine Weissenberg with whom he eventually had three children.

SUCCESS

Mount Johnson is where Johnson established a thriving fur trade business which would soon make him a very wealthy man indeed. A key to Johnson's amazing success was his ability to see some political and cultural issues from the Native American point of view and convey that perspective to them. He also learned the Mohawk language and customs. The Indians trusted Johnson more than any other white man and were eager to bring their furs to him. These Indians were mostly from the Iroquois confederacy, especially Mohawks, and they named Johnson "Warraghiyagey," which means "man who does much business."

Johnson continued to grow his business, increase his wealth and landholdings, and interact positively with the Indians, throughout the 1740s and 1750s. At this period of history England and France were in constant struggles to control North America. Johnson's positive influence with the Iroquois was noted by the English governors. In 1754 he was a valued participant in a "congress" at Albany which was held to formulate a British policy toward the Indians. In 1755 Johnson was appointed the influential and important position of superintendent of Indian Affairs in lands to the north of the Ohio River.

THE FRENCH AND INDIAN WAR

The French and Indian War, from 1754 to 1763, was the final war between England and France for control of North America. Sir William Johnson played an important part in the British victory. His Indian diplomacy skills convinced the Iroquois to participate in the war on the side of the English. In August 1755, Johnson was in charge of 1,500 Colonial troops and 200 Mohawk Indians. The entire force was encamped on the southern shore of Lake George (recently named Lake George by William Johnson). Johnson's intention was to advance north with his forces and capture the French Fort St. Frederick located on the Crown Point Peninsula. On September 8, 1755, French forces under the leadership of Baron de Dieskau took the initiative and attacked a contingent of Johnson's forces who were heading for Fort Edward. After initially falling back to their camp, the English rallied behind reinforcements from the camp and turned a possible defeat into victory at the Battle of Lake George. The French had to withdraw back to Fort St. Frederick. Johnson was a hero for stopping the French from invading any farther south. Afterward Johnson supervised the building of Fort William Henry on the site of his Lake George encampment.

Later in the war (1759) Johnson and his Iroquois were part of a British siege at the very important French-held Fort Niagara. When the British commander was killed by friendly fire, Johnson took charge and managed to capture the fort for the British.

The French and Indian war ended in 1763 with the signing of the Treaty of Paris in which France gave up all claims in North America. As a result of his important contributions to the English victory in the war, Johnson was given a barony and was ever after referred to as Sir William Johnson.

A SUITABLE HOME

Johnson had been contemplating the creation of a large home suitable for his position as a wealthy fur trader, landowner, and Indian diplomat, at least since the early 1760s. On May 10, 1763, construction began on Johnson Hall. The plans were Johnson's (some sources indicate Johnson consulted an architect), and he utilized the most popular construction style at that time, Georgian. The builder was a respected man named Samuel Fuller, and the house became one of the finest mansions in all of New York. As we have seen, the property eventually became a self-contained estate with a sawmill, gristmill, gardens, blacksmith shop, storage areas, gun shop, and other useful structures and facilities.

SUPERINTENDANT OF INDIAN AFFAIRS

Sir William Johnson continued on as superintendent of Indian Affairs for the rest of his life. He reinforced his role of superintendent by sometimes acting as an advocate for Indian interests, as well as for British concerns. Johnson's postwar dealings with the Indians had a significant impact on westward expansion of the colonies. In 1766 Johnson negotiated a treaty with the rebelling Ottawa Indian leader named Pontiac. This laid the groundwork for British expansion into the formerly French-held Great Lakes Region. Sir William also presided over the Council of Fort Stanwix in 1768 during which the Iroquois gave up claims to land which eventually became Kentucky.

Johnson Hall became the site of numerous large gatherings with Native Americans, including the traditional gift-giving fair. Here is where the British government would distribute gifts to the Iroquois. Johnson would arrange various activities such as greased pig contests and races to entertain and foster a community-like feeling between the English and the Indians.

Sir William also planned to found a town, called Johnstown, named after his son. To further this project, Johnson built a school, a church, and a courthouse.

SUDDEN DEATH

In July 1774, at Johnson Hall Sir William was addressing a large gathering of about six hundred Indians when he collapsed and died of a stroke at the age of fifty-nine.

Johnson's holdings went to his son John for a short while. John Johnson was a Tory, loyal to the British cause during the Revolutionary War, and thus his property was confiscated by New York State at the end of the war. In 1779 Johnson Hall was sold to a Silas Talbot. This extensive property remained in private hands for many years until New York State reacquired it in 1906. Throughout the years of private ownership Johnson Hall underwent many modifications. Fortunately the State has restored much of Johnson Hall back to its 1763 look and feel. In 1960 Johnson Hall was declared a national historic landmark.

A visit to Johnson Hall State Historic Site makes it easy for us to picture the hall overlooking a large crowd of Native Americans performing dances and ceremonies, and there is no doubt that Sir William Johnson will be giving a speech and joining the frenetic festivities. We are so fortunate to have Johnson Hall to serve as a glimpse back in time to the amazing eighteenth century world of Sir William Johnson.

VII.

Fort William Henry Museum and Restoration

Fort William Henry. Photo credit Carl Heilman
II. Courtesy Fort William Henry Museum.

Location: 48 Canada Street (Route 9) Lake George, New York 12845

Directions: Take Interstate 87 to exit Number 21 (Route 9) toward Lake George village. Fort is on north side of the road. Park behind the Village Blacksmith Steakhouse, or at the Fort William Henry Conference Center.

Coordinates: 43.42028 N, -73.71111 W

Season: May to third week in October. 9:00 am – 5:00 pm daily. Summer hours may be extended, call to be sure.

Admission: Moderate fee. Child and senior discount.

Current and past military personnel and residents of Lake George – free (Individual only)

Contacts:

Phone: (518)688-5471

Web: http://www.fwhmuseum.com

DESCRIPTION

Fort William Henry Museum is an important recreation of a short-lived but almost legendary eighteenth century fort located at the south end of Lake George. The siege of Fort William Henry in 1757 by French General Marquis de Montcalm is the background for much of James Fennimore Cooper's immortal novel *The Last of the Mohicans*. Today's fort is a faithful replica of the original and serves as a museum whose displays tell the dramatic story of the forts' two years of tumultuous existence and illustrates life during the French and Indian War.

Fort William Henry Museum was built in the 1950s on the site of the original fort. Visitors are encouraged to take the guided tour of the museum. These tours are offered every hour on the hour with the last tour beginning at 4:00 pm. Your guide will be dressed in a period appropriate military costume and will explain the weapons and tactics of eighteenth century warfare. In addition there will be live firing demonstrations of muskets and cannons, along with a demonstration of musket ball molding. After the tour, visitors can take a self-guided tour of the museums many exhibits.

The reconstructed fort is made of logs, has four sides, and has a point-like projection from each corner called a bastion. Bastions allow defenders the ability to fire their rifles and cannons parallel to the walls in defense of the fort. Inside the fort are several two-story log structures which served as barracks. Also there is a central parade ground and a number of cannons including some originals that were found in Lake George. There are also collections of period artifacts and archeological findings.

The museum is intended to be family friendly, and after the guided tour, children are invited to join the Kings Army. The new "soldiers" are given a uniform, a musket, and a chance to drill with the guide. Participants are given a certificate signing them up as soldiers and a coin for payment.

After checking out the museum, visitors may stop at the Sutler Shoppe (inside the fort) for a large selection of Fort William Henry and Lake George souvenirs. Included are books, toys, quality replica muskets and cannons, along with clothing, candy, and other gifts. Note that fort admission is not required in order to enter the Sutter's Shoppe.

BRIEF HISTORY

Fort William Henry is famous quite beyond its historical impact for several reasons. First, it was the site of significant atrocities committed by Indians (and allowed by some of the French soldiers) after the fort was surrendered by the English to the French in 1757. Secondly, the fort is the backdrop of the classic novel *The Last of the Mohicans*, written by James Fennimore Cooper. Finally, Fort William Henry was part of a system of English forts utilized during the French and Indian War. Its capture by the French, in 1757, represented the high water mark of French success in a war they would eventually lose.

GEOGRAPHY AND ANCIENT HISTORY

The locations of many historical sites that we see today are areas that have been used by humans for a very long time, sometimes even before recorded history. This is usually because of the beneficial geographical features of the area, such as a proximity to waterways, high defensible ground, or nearness to a food source. This phenomenon is true of the location of Fort William Henry at the bottom (south shore) of Lake George. This site had ready access to Lake George, for water, boat access, and defense, and it was on a small rise which aided its defensibility. Archeological evidence (some of which the museum displays) indicates that this site was used by many different groups of humans at least as far back as 3500 BC. At the time that the early European visitors first saw the lake, in the early 1600s, the area was claimed by both the Mohicans and the Iroquois (especially the Mohawks). By the time the French and Indian War began in 1754, this area was claimed by the English.

STRATEGIC LOCATION DURING THE FRENCH AND INDIAN WAR

The French and Indian War was the final of a series of world wars between France and England for control of North America. The two countries had been clashing militarily off and on for nearly one hundred years in this struggle. The French and Indian War, beginning in 1754, would settle the issue for good with a British victory. The war ended officially with the signing of the Treaty of Paris in 1763 in which France gave up all its territory in North America.

One of the critical strategic areas that both the French and the English coveted was the water route corridor from the Hudson River all the way to Canada. The route consisted of a trip up the Hudson River to a relatively short portage at "The Great Carrying Place," then on to Lake George, to Lake Champlain, and finally to the St. Lawrence River. This route was especially critical because the English were gradually moving north from Albany while the French were moving south from Montreal and Quebec. Whoever could control access to Lake Champlain and /or Lake George could control these important invasion routes.

FORT EDWARD IS BUILT

In 1755 Captain Robert Rogers began work on a fortified storehouse at the portage from the Hudson River to Wood Creek (the aforementioned "Great Carrying Place," which led into Lake Champlain). In July 1755, British Colonel William Johnson and his forces arrived to finish work on the fort, which eventually became Fort Edward, which at that time was the northernmost British fort. Next Johnson, with intentions to eventually stage an attack on French Fort St. Frederick (located at "the Narrows" of Lake Champlain), traveled to the southern end of Lac du Saint Sacrament, and renamed it Lake George.

BATTLE OF LAKE GEORGE

Johnson and his men began work on a fortified camp at the southwest corner of the lake in August of 1755. On September 8, French forces, originally planning to attack Fort Edward, decided instead to attack Johnson's forces at Lake George. The French set up an ambush on the road leading from Johnson's camp to Fort Edward. A portion of Johnson's men who were on a scout toward Fort Edward that morning stumbled in to the French ambush and a furious fight ensued. Things went poorly for the English, but they retreated in good order, back to their military camp at Lake George. Here they were reinforced by reserves from the camp and staged a successful counterattack. The French ended up fleeing for their lives and Colonel Johnson became a hero. The two phases of the day's action are called the "Bloody Morning Scout" and the "Battle of Bloody Pond" or together, the Battle of Lake George. After the battle Johnson ordered the building of a fort next to their fortified camp. This fort would be called Fort William Henry, and by November 13, 1755, it was ready for occupancy.

FORT WILLIAM HENRY IS BUILT

The design and construction of Fort William Henry was overseen by a British military engineer named William Eyre. The resulting fort featured four slightly irregular sides surrounding a central parade ground. Bastions on each corner of the fort allowed parallel firing along the walls. The walls were constructed by erecting log facings thirty feet apart and filling the space between with dirt. Inside the fort were wooden barracks two stories high. There was a powder magazine located in the northeast bastion and a hospital in the south bastion. A dry moat surrounded the fort on three sides while the fourth side sloped down to Lake George. Access to the fort was by a bridge across the moat. Fort William Henry was only capable of housing between four hundred and five hundred soldiers, so an entrenched camp was constructed about 750 yards to the southwest. The fort was garrisoned by several companies of Roger's Rangers and British Regulars of the forty-fourth foot. William Eyre was in command of the fort.

COLONEL MONRO TAKES COMMAND

The year 1756 was relatively quiet year at Fort William Henry as far as any major battles were concerned. Instead the year featured small-scale raids by both sides in the Lake George sector of the French and Indian War. However, 1757 brought renewed activity. In addition to both the French and the British building up their forces in the area, the French had built a fort on the strategically desirable Ticonderoga Peninsula and called it Fort Carillon. In March of 1757 the French launched an unsuccessful attack on Fort William Henry, just managing to burn some boats and destroy some minor property. In spring of 1757 command of Fort William Henry was given to Lieutenant Colonel George Monro, and the garrison numbers had swelled to around 2,300 men, many of whom were stationed in the outlying camp. Unfortunately many of the men in both the fort and the camp were sick at that time, some with smallpox.

The English military goal had been to capture Fort St. Frederick at Crown Point, but now the French had built and garrisoned Fort Carillon (the French name for Fort Ticonderoga), and this fort would have to be taken first. However, before the English could act, the

French decided on a preemptive strike, and a plan was drawn up to capture Fort William Henry and perhaps Fort Edward too.

THE MARQUIS DE MONTCALM CAPTURES THE FORT

At this time (summer 1757), the Marquis de Montcalm was the commander-in-chief of French military forces in North America, and plans were made to attack Fort William Henry. On August 3, 1757, General Montcalm arrived in the vicinity of Fort William Henry with eight thousand men and set up his siege camps to the south and west of the fort. Colonel Monro sent dispatches to General Webb of Fort Edward requesting reinforcements. Meanwhile, General Montcalm's siege operations progressed nearer and nearer to Fort William Henry. The two sides exchanged artillery and small arms fire until August 7. At that time the French, under a flag of truce, presented a note to Colonel Monro that they had intercepted from General Webb of Fort Edward. The note told Monro that General Webb would not be sending any relief forces to Fort William Henry. Vastly outnumbered and outgunned, Colonel Monro knew that he had to surrender to the French, although he held out for one more day. The British surrendered early on in the morning of August 9.

General Montcalm had promised the British, and their camp followers, that they would all be allowed to withdraw to Fort Edward with a French escort. The British soldiers would be allowed full honors of war provided they would refrain from participating in the war for eighteen months. In addition, the British could keep their muskets, although they would not be allowed to have any ammunition. In return, the British promised to release French prisoners within three months.

MASSACRE

General Montcalm was concerned about his Indian allies upholding the terms of the surrender. He knew the Indians would be angry about the lack of booty and scalps that had been promised them earlier in order to get them to participate in the attack. Out of

Montcalm's total force of eight thousand, some two thousand were Native Americans. The general went to the chiefs of the various tribes, explained the terms of the surrender to them, and asked them to restrain their braves from looting and havoc. This did not work.

Early on August 9, after surrendering, the British were moved out of the fort to the entrenched camp. This left about seventy British sick and wounded in the fort at the mercy of the French and their Indian allies. Almost immediately the Indians entered the fort and began to plunder what baggage was left inside. Soon cries and screams for help were heard coming from the fort. Many of the helpless sick and wounded left in the fort were butchered and scalped. One Indian emerged from the fort carrying the severed head of one of the British wounded. At this point, some semblance of order was restored by the French. Estimates of the number of wounded and sick killed by the Indians after the surrender, vary widely, but it seems likely that at least a dozen were killed in this preliminary phase of the massacre.

The tribes were now restless and lingering around the fort and the camp, creating a volatile situation. A planned march from the entrenched camp to Fort Edward was postponed until the next morning as many Indians had gathered in the area.

After a tense night, the British formed to leave, with Colonel Monro on horseback leading the way. Montcalm assigned an escort of two hundred French soldiers to protect the British on their march. However, just as the last British left the camp, the Indians descended on seventeen helpless wounded who had been left in camp huts. All seventeen wounded were killed; then the Indians began attacking the rear of the British column, taking clothing and other belongings, and killing and scalping as they went. In addition to the murdering, many captives were taken by the Indians, including children torn from their mother's arms. Some of the French soldiers tried to stop the carnage while others did not. Many of the British soldiers broke ranks and tried to escape through the woods. Many were pursued and killed. Eventually Montcalm and his men were able to restore a semblance of order, and the majority of the English prisoners made it to Fort Edward. A number of the men who had fled continued to straggle in to Fort Edward for days.

No one knows how many English were killed in the massacre. Estimates vary widely. Some of the captives taken that day were later ransomed back to the English. It is reported that the atrocities bothered Montcalm for the rest of his days (which weren't all that many). Once all the surviving English had left, the French burned Fort William Henry to the ground.

THANKFULLY THE MUSEUM ENDURES

Today the Fort William Henry Museum stands on the site of the original fort. Nearby is a state historical marker's where the entrenched camp was located. The site of Fort Edward is marked only by a couple of blue signs.

The important Fort William Henry Museum and Restoration provides a fascinating look into a mid-eighteenth century North American fort and tells the story of a tragic incident in the French and Indian War.

VIII.

Saratoga Battlefield National Historical Park

Saratoga Battlefield overlooking the Hudson River.
Photo courtesy the National Park Service.

Location: Saratoga National Historic Park, 648 Route 32, Stillwater, NY 12170

Directions: These directions will get you to the visitors' center. See below for directions to Victory Woods, the monument and the Schuyler House.

> **From the South** – take "Northway," I-87, to exit 12. Turn right to follow Route 67 eastbound. Stay right to go through two traffic circles. After second traffic circle, get in left lane for third traffic circle. Take third exit, US Route 9 north. Go 1.6 miles and turn right onto Route 9 p. Go 4.5 miles, and then turn right on Route 423. Go 5.5 miles to Route 32. Turn left and go about two miles to Battlefield entrance. Visitors' center is just uphill from the parking lot.

> **From North** – Take I-87 south to exit 14. Take Route 29 east into Schuylerville. At US Route 4 (a T intersection) take a right (Broad Street and Route 4 south). Go eight miles south to Park entrance on right. Go two miles to Regular Parking and Visitors' Center.

> **From East or West** – Take Route 29 to Schuylerville. At T intersection with Route 4 (Broad Street) turn South on Route 4 for eight miles to the Park entrance road (less than one-fifth mile if you came from the east), and then two miles to the visitors center

Note: The next three parts of the park are external to the main battlefield site.

Saratoga Monument – Eight miles north of the battlefield off US Route 4 (Broad Street) just south of Schuylerville Burgoyne Road, to Monument Drive take three-fourth miles.

Victory Woods – Just one-half mile from the Saratoga Monument. Again from US Route 4, take Burgoyne Road (County Road 338) about two-third miles to Monument Drive. Victory Woods is at the end of Monument Drive or you can walk to it from the Monument itself.

Schuyler House – Located in Schuylerville on US Route 4 just south of the small bridge. It is a large yellow house.

GPS Coordinates: 43.013834 N, -73.651271 W

Season: Battlefield – Pedestrian use seven days week, all year to sunset
Tour Road – March 31 – November 30 weather permitting.
Closed Thanksgiving Day

9:00 am – 4:00 pm November
9:00 am – 5:00 pm April, October
9:00 am – 7:00 pm May 1, Labor Day
9:00 am – 6:00 pm September

Visitors' Center – 9:00 am – 5:00 pm seven days week except
Thanksgiving, Christmas, New Year's Day
Schuyler House – Memorial through Labor Day, Wednesday
through Sunday. Forty minute tours scheduled at 9:00
am, 9:45 am, 10:30 am, 11:45 am, 12:30 pm, 1:15 pm,
2:00 pm, 2:45 pm, 3:30 pm, and 4:15 pm. Labor Day –
Third weekend in October only open for weekends.
Saratoga Monument – Memorial Day through Labor Day,
Wednesday through Sunday, 9:30 am – 4:45 pm. Labor
Day – Third weekend October, weekends only.
Victory Woods – Seven days a week sunrise to sunset, path not
maintained in winter.

Admission: Season May 1 to October 31. Fees accepted only by
cash, check. Modest fee for cars, less for bikes. Fee is valid for
seven days.
Note: Check the National Park Service Web site for NPS America
the Beautiful yearlong passes and senior passes.
Contact: Web: - http:///www.nps.sara/index.htm

DESCRIPTION

Saratoga Battlefield National Historic Park preserves the site of the
two battles of Saratoga, which are often considered by historians to
be among the top fifteen most important battles in the history of the
world. The setting is the American Revolutionary War, and the loca-

tion is an area along the upper Hudson River in Upstate New York. There are actually two battles of Saratoga between the Americans and the British; they occurred on September 19, 1777, and October 7, 1777. The National Park preserves the main battlefield area as well as three auxiliary (outside the main park) sites: the Saratoga Monument, the Schuyler House, and Victory Woods. We will present the four sites separately beginning with the battlefield itself.

It is suggested (but by no means necessary) that you start your exploring at the Visitors' Center (which is two miles from the entrance on Route 4). It is also suggested that you pick up a map and park brochure at the Visitors' Center, since the park is very large, with much to see. Also, you can use the restrooms, visit the book and gift shop, watch a twenty-minute orientation film, view a fiber-optic light map, and peruse the interesting artifacts which are on display.

The essential method of exploring the battlefield is via the tour road. This is a one-way toll road (covered by your entrance fee) which is more than nine miles long and features ten tour stops. Tour stops are the locations of interpretive markers which help you understand how the two battles unfolded and what part of them you are looking at. Please note that bicycles are welcome on the tour road as are horses, and there are walking trails too.

SCHUYLER HOUSE:

This is the restored country house of the important American General Phillip Schuyler and is located eight miles north of the battlefield on US Route 4. Check above for hours that the Schuyler House is open as they are somewhat limited, but a tour of this interesting site is free and guided.

SARATOGA MONUMENT:

Saratoga Monument is a 155-foot-high obelisk that celebrates the American victory at Saratoga. It is also about eight miles north of the battlefield. Check above for the hours that it is open since currently it is only open Wednesdays through Sundays during the season.

VICTORY WOODS:

Victory Woods is a new (opened in 2010) addition to the park. It is eight and one half miles north of the battlefield, about one-half mile from Saratoga Monument. The Woods marks the site of the camp wherein General Burgoyne got himself completely surrounded by the Americans as he was retreating from the Americans following the second Battle of Saratoga. Here he was forced to surrender his forces to General Horatio Gates.

Victory Woods is twenty-two acres and is situated, appropriately enough in the town of Victory. Visitors can park at Saratoga Monument and walk a trail through the cemetery to the Victory Woods trail head, or drive to the end of Monument Drive and park there. There is a boardwalk and trail that runs one-half mile through the woods and features interpretive placards that tell the story of General Burgoyne's last stand. Victory Woods is open every day, but there is no trail maintenance during the winter.

BRIEF HISTORY

Following is a brief history of the two battles of Saratoga. The battles are interesting, important, and involved. It is suggested that if you have the time and inclination, reading a full-length account of the battles could enhance your enjoyment of the site.

THE PLAN

By 1777, the two-year point in the Revolutionary War, the British had decided that they must split the American Colonies into two sections, in order to isolate New England. They figured that by isolating the most passionate region of the "rebellion," New England, they could concentrate their efforts there and bring about a quicker end to the war. In addition, the middle and southern colonies were not so urgently rebellious, having a higher percentage of Loyalists than New England.

To isolate New England, the British planned a three-pronged movement of troops to converge in the vicinity of Albany. One British army, commanded by General Howe, would proceed up the Hudson River from New York City. The main British force, commanded by General John Burgoyne, would head south from Montreal and proceed along the Lake Champlain, Lake George, Hudson River corridor, to Albany. The third British force was led by Colonel Barry St. Leger in an attempt to support Burgoyne and protect his western flank. St. Leger would head east from Oswego to Wood Creek, to the Mohawk River, and then join Burgoyne somewhere along the Hudson River. These movements, executed successfully, would isolate New England from the rest of the colonies and allow the British to concentrate their forces against the most ardent revolutionaries, those in the New England area.

WHAT HAPPENED – THE FIRST BATTLE

Recall that General Burgoyne was to move his army south from Montreal intending to exert British control over the Lake Champlain, Lake George, Hudson River corridor, and meet up with the other two British armies in the Albany area. By the beginning of August 1777, Burgoyne had reached Fort Edward, a supply fort overlooking a bend in the Hudson River about fifteen miles from Lake George. Along the way his forces had captured Fort Ticonderoga, defeated, fleeing American forces at Hubbardston, Vermont, and set up a supply line in the wake of his advances.

Burgoyne would spend the month of August at Fort Edward. During that time a very ominous event occurred, perhaps portending disasters to come for Burgoyne's army. Burgoyne ordered a force of about eight hundred German mercenaries to proceed to a strategic location in Bennington, Vermont. Before the Germans could get to their destination they encountered American Militia soldiers just west of Bennington. The Americans thoroughly defeated the Germans, capturing or killing nearly the entire force. To make matters worse for Burgoyne, the defeat at Bennington convinced many of his Indian allies to depart for home.

More bad news was soon to reach General Burgoyne, this time from Colonel Barry St. Leger. St. Leger had been working his way south and east from Oswego toward a rendezvous with Burgoyne along the Hudson River near Albany. On August 6 St. Leger's forces met a strong American force in the Battle of Oriskany. General Nicholas Herkimer's American forces were forced to withdraw at the end of the day, but so were the British. This in conjunction with St. Leger's inability to capture Fort Stanwix, caused St. Leger to abandon his mission and retreat all the way back into Canada. This unwelcome news reached General Burgoyne on August 28.

Still more bad news had reached Burgoyne earlier in August. General Howe, who was to have led British forces north from New York City to join up with Burgoyne, decided to head south instead, in order to capture Philadelphia. This decision was made for the purpose of distracting George Washington's army away from recapturing New York City. Howe's departure from New York left General Henry Clinton in charge. Since Howe took a significant army to Philadelphia, Clinton now had a much reduced force with which to eventually meet up with Burgoyne.

In early September General Burgoyne's situation was getting desperate, and the British plan to isolate New England was falling apart. With the beginning of fall now upon him, Burgoyne needed to decide where to establish his winter quarters. He could retrace his steps back to Fort Ticonderoga or move ahead to Albany. Burgoyne made the fatal decision to move south along the Hudson River toward Albany. By mid-September Burgoyne was on the west bank of the Hudson just north of Saratoga.

THE AMERICANS

The American forces had been moving south in the face of Burgoyne's advance ever since Burgoyne had captured Fort Ticonderoga. However, the American forces were growing in number with the arrival of state militias. Also, General Washington had sent reinforcements to Gates, in the form of officers, including the very important Major General Benedict Arnold, and more militia, including Daniel

Morgan's sharpshooters. On August 19 General Philip Schuyler was replaced by General Horatio Gates as overall commander of American Forces in the northern area.

In early September Gates had moved north and began constructing strong defensive work on high ground along the west bank of the Hudson River known as Bemis Heights. Gates defensive works were able to control the only road south to Albany, which ran along the river. The defensive lines also extended west and south to prevent Burgoyne from circumventing the defensive works on their western flank. In essence, the Americans now blocked the British from any further movement to the south.

THE FIRST BATTLE OF SARATOGA

By the middle of September General Burgoyne was moving cautiously south. On September 18 his advance guard, now just four miles from the American Lines, made contact with American scouting parties in a series of skirmishes.

The next day (September 19) Burgoyne ordered an advance of his forces in three columns. Along the River road he sent German troops, along with British infantry, under the command of Baron Riedesel (this constituted the British left). The British center column was led by General Hamilton, and the British right column was led by General Simon Fraser. By 10:00 am all three British columns were advancing.

A key position on the battlefront was the American left wing, on wooded high ground to the northwest of Bemis Heights. Gates sent Daniel Morgan's sharpshooters as well as some infantry units to the northwest to intercept the British in that area. Although much of the ground to the west was thickly wooded, there was a large open field there which was part of John Freeman's farm.

As the British advanced into the open field, Morgan's men attacked, picking off many British officers. British reinforcements drove Morgan's men back. Then American reinforcements, sent by Gates, allowed the Americans to advance, at one point temporarily capturing some of the British artillery. The battle continued to ebb and flow until British reinforcements from Riedesel finally allowed the British to push the Americans back to the woods at sundown. The British had control of the battlefield but had received many more casualties than the Americans, and their march toward Albany had been stopped cold.

Now the two armies facing each other settled in to a holding period, with light skirmishing daily, but no major contact. Burgoyne was in communication with General Clinton in New York City, hoping that Clinton would reinforce him or at least create a diversion to amuse the Americans. Burgoyne's supplies were rapidly dwindling while he waited. The Americans, however, were receiving both men, in the form of militia, and supplies. By early October, Gate's American forces numbered over 12,000 men, while Burgoyne's forces were less than six thousand men, and they were running out of food.

Burgoyne and the British had now reached a crisis point. They were low on supplies, facing a superior and well-defended army, and it was clear that no relief was going to come to them from the south. They could either retreat back to the north or try to get past the American defenses and proceed to the south. Although some of his officers wanted to retreat back the way they had come, Burgoyne would not hear of it. They would move ahead and assault the Americans left with a force of two thousand men.

THE SECOND BATTLE OF SARATOGA

General Gates and the other American officers knew that Burgoyne was in big trouble. British deserters had relayed to the Americans all the British problems with regard to their situation. It is interesting to note that General Gates had just removed General Benedict Arnold from field command due to an apparent conflict of egos. However, as we shall see, Arnold had his own ideas with regard to his participation in the upcoming events. Nevertheless, Gates put himself in charge of the critical American left and placed General Lincoln in charge of the right.

THE BRITISH ATTACK

About 10:00 am on October 7 Burgoyne began to move artillery and two thousand men toward the American left as a reconnaissance in force. In a short while they arrived at some high ground located on a local farm (Barber's wheat field) where they halted in order to observe the American position. Soon American scouts brought news of the British advance to General Gates. Gates reacted by ordering Daniel Morgan's sharpshooters, and a number of other units, out to reinforce the American left.

The attack on the American left began at 2:00 pm. British grenadiers began shooting at and then charging the Americans. The Americans responded strongly and soon had devastated the grenadiers. The action was a total rout. Quickly the action shifted farther out on the American left. Here British General Fraser, escorted by Canadians and Indians, attempted to move west in order to outflank the Americans. Daniel Morgan's men brushed aside the Canadians and the Indians, and were soon engaged against Fraser's regulars. In the furious action, Fraser was killed and his men began a hasty, disorganized retreat. The entire British advance was rapidly crumbling, as all units endeavored to make their way back to their entrenchments.

GENERAL BENEDICT ARNOLD
DISOBEYS ORDERS AND JOINS IN

At this point General Benedict Arnold, who had been ordered to stay in camp, disobeyed those orders and rode out to join the action. The British had two battlefield fortifications, known as Balcarre's redoubt and Breymann's redoubt, near the west side of their camp, which they now desperately tried to hold. General Arnold led an attack on the stronger of the two redoubts, Balcarre's, but the British held. Arnold, seeing that the British were too strong here, rode to Breymann's redoubt, risking his life, and joined the furious attack there. Morgan's men had surrounded Breymann, who was killed, and soon captured the redoubt. Unfortunately, General Arnold was shot near the end of the attack and his leg was broken. Arnold was carried back to the American camp on a litter as darkness began to settle over the battlefield.

A BRITISH DISASTER

The Americans had won the day in a very decisive way. Between the two battles of Saratoga Burgoyne had lost one thousand men while the Americans had lost five hundred. In addition, the British had lost one of their most popular generals in Simon Fraser. Burgoyne was now outnumbered three to one. That night Burgoyne began retreating back the way he had come, to the north. By October 13, he was at Saratoga and completely surrounded. On October 17 he surrendered his entire army to General Gates.

The upstart Americans had won a very decisive victory over the best-trained and equipped regular army in the world. The victory encouraged France to join the war on the side of the Americans, providing much needed supplies, moral support, and leaders. It is ironic that one of the main driving forces in this great victory, General Arnold, would later turn against his country and join the British, and the winning general, Horatio Gates, would go on to embarrass himself as a coward in the disastrous loss at the battle of Camden.

GENERAL BENEDICT ARNOLD
RIGHTFULLY HONORED

On the battlefield of Saratoga there is a "Boot Monument" dedicated to "the most brilliant soldier of the Continental Army." It is to commemorate General Benedict Arnold (for obvious reasons his name is not on the monument) and marks the spot where Arnold was shot in the leg on October 7.

A visit to Saratoga Battle National Historic Park is an unforgettable experience. Visitors get to see the fields and woods where General Gates's (and General Benedict Arnold's) ragtag Americans thoroughly defeated the highly disciplined British Regular army in one of the most important battles in the history of the world.

IX.

Fort Ticonderoga

Fort Ticonderoga. Photo Carl Heilman II.
Courtesy Fort Ticonderoga Museum.

Location: 30 Fort Ti Road, Ticonderoga, New York, 12283

Directions: From US Interstate 87 (North or South), take Exit 28 onto NY Routes 22 and 74 East. Follow for about eighteen miles. Turn left onto Route 74 East. Follow for about a half mile and the entrance to Fort Ticonderoga will be on the right.

From NY Route 9-N (North or South), follow 9-N to the traffic circle in the town of Ticonderoga. Turn east onto Montcalm Street and continue three miles through two stop-lights and one flashing light onto Route 74 East. Follow for about a halfmile and the entrance to Fort Ticonderoga will be on the right.

From Vermont, follow state Route 74 West to the Ticonderoga Ferry (toll ferry) at Shoreham or Route 22A via Route 73 in Orwell. After crossing Lake Champlain, the main entrance to the Fort will be one mile ahead on the left.

Coordinates: 43.84167° N, -73.3875°W

Season: Mid-May to Late October (specific dates change by year, check Web site) 9:30 am to 5:00 pm (last ticket 4:30 pm)

Admission: Moderate fee. Discounts for children, seniors

Contact: Fort Ticonderoga
PO Box 390
Ticonderoga, NY 12283
Phone: 518/585-2821
e-mail: info@fort-ticonderoga.org
Web: www.fort-ticonderoga.org

DESCRIPTION

Fort Ticonderoga is a magnificent restored eighteenth century star-shaped military fort situated on more than two thousand acres of land, on the west shore of and near the south end of Lake Champlain. This is one of the most important historic sites in North America. Situated on the Ticonderoga Peninsula, the fort overlooks both water entrances (the La Chute River and Wood Creek) into southern Lake Champlain. This was an extremely strategic location during the eighteenth and nineteenth centuries, providing for potential military control of an important north/south travel route. Standing nearly anywhere at the fort and looking at the incredible view of the south end of Lake Champlain, a visitor can see with their own eyes the military value of the location.

Fort Ticonderoga is managed by a private foundation and consists of the magnificent stone fort itself, a wonderful museum, store, research center, and several important landmarks in the surrounding area. The landmarks include Mount Defiance, Mount Hope, Mount Independence, and the Carillon Battlefield (a half mile west of the fort). The Carillon Battlefield contains the oldest (mid-eighteenth century) untouched earthworks in North America. In addition, there are some impressive gardens on display at the fort.

Each day there are numerous demonstrations of eighteenth century fort life. Visitors can participate in guided tours, watch musket demonstrations, or view other depictions of daily solder life at the fort. There are even fife and drum concerts to entertain.

The nationally important museum which is housed in the restored 1756 soldiers' barracks and changing exhibition space in the museum's education center display period weapons, art, and many other fascinating artifacts.

The store has a good selection of history books, gifts, souvenirs, and food.

A site admission fee is captured at the entrance to the property and includes access to the entire site, fort, gardens, and French defensive lines (still visible today after more than 250 years). Daily programs also take place at the top of Mount Defiance, which affords breathtaking views of the surrounding scenery. A nominal fee fess is charged to access that site.

BRIEF HISTORY

GEOGRAPHY

The word "Ticonderoga" is derived from an Iroquois word meaning "it is at the junction of two waterways." Actually there are three bodies of water near the Ticonderoga peninsula, which is situated on the west shore near the southern end of Lake Champlain. These waterways are the lake itself, South Bay (actually a fingerlike part of the lake to the southeast), and the LaChute River, also known as Ticonderoga Creek, which enters the lake from the southwest. The LaChute River is the outlet from Lake George which is three and one-half miles to the south. The Hudson River, Lake George, Lake Champlain, and the Richelieu River form a water route from New York City all the way to the St. Lawrence River with just a few short portages along the way. This route was used by Native Americans for centuries before European contact. For Europeans also it was the only practical means of travel between French Canada (along the St. Lawrence River) and the English colonies to the south. The strategically located Ticonderoga Peninsula overlooks both entrances to the southern end of Lake Champlain, as well as the narrow southern end of the lake itself.

EARLY HISTORY

The first of a number of historic events to occur on the Ticonderoga peninsula happened on July 30, 1609. Samuel de Champlain, two other Frenchmen, and sixty Algonquian warriors, clashed with two hundred Iroquois warriors (mostly Mohawk). Though outnumbered, Champlain and his Indian allies won the battle after killing several Iroquois chiefs with there never before seen (or heard) harquebus (matchlock muskets). Champlain and his Algonquians returned to Canada, but this event had a negative impact on French/Iroquois relations for many decades.

The first known European to traverse the portage from Lake George to Lake Champlain (along the La Chute River because the river has many rapids) was a Jesuit missionary named Isaac Jogues. The year was 1642, and Jogues was attempting to escape a battle between the Iroquois and the Huron.

The next development at Ticonderoga occurred in 1691 when Pieter Schuyler built a small wooden fort there. Schuyler's fort was an attempt to prevent French and Indian raiding parties from travelling farther south into British territory.

The conflicts between the French and the English, and their Indian allies, continued sporadically through the seventeenth and into the eighteenth century. These conflicts took the form of raids and small clashes often against settlements (and often against non-combatants). The culmination of the growing tension between these two powers is called the French and Indian war. This war was ignited in 1754 by a small battle in Pennsylvania involving militia Lieutenant Colonel George Washington and ended with the British in control of North America. Fort Ticonderoga was built by the

French during this war and played an important role in it, as well as the Revolutionary War.

The year is 1755, the French and Indian war is a full blown world war, and the Lake George, Lake Champlain corridor is of crucial importance to both the French and the English. The French are ensconced at Fort St. Frederick, on the western shore of Lake Champlain, about eleven miles north of the site of the future Fort Ticonderoga. The British are stationed directly to the south at the foot of Lake George and are building Fort William Henry on the south shore. In between the two forces is a critical point of land that could control all north south travel along the corridor. It is, of course, the Ticonderoga Peninsula. Both sides recognize its strategic value and want to erect a fort on this point, but the French are much closer and better prepared to do so.

CONSTRUCTION BEGINS

In 1755 the governor of New France (Canada) was the Marquis de Vaudreuil. On a crisp September day Vaudreuil sent thirty-two–year-old Lieutenant Sieur de Lotbiniere, of the royal engineers, to the Ticonderoga Peninsula, and ordered him to erect fortifications there. By October 17 Lotbiniere's large workforce (troops from Fort St. Frederick and from Canada) had cleared enough ground to trace out the fort and had begun digging the foundation. The temporary name of the emerging structure was Fort Vaudreuil. Later it would be called Fort Carillon by the French, and still later Fort Ticonderoga by the English. By February 1756, the fort, though incomplete, was capable of defending itself. Further developments in 1756 were the building of a sawmill on the La Chute River, and the construction, inside the fort, of stone barracks capable of housing up to five hundred men. In addition, external guard posts were erected, along with a redoubt and basic fortifications at the outlet from Lake George (the source of the La Chute River). Work on the fort itself continued on into 1758 when the barracks and demi-lunes (triangular-shaped defenses in front of a fort's wall) were completed.

The four-sided Fort Carillon is based on a design by a highly regarded French military engineer named Vauban. There were four-pointed projections (bastions), one for each corner of the fort. The walls were seven feet high and fourteen feet thick. They were made from squared wooden timbers serving as a framework and then filled in with earth. Shortly after the walls were completed, the French began dressing their outer sides with stones mined from a nearby quarry. Construction inside the fort was of stone and consisted of three barracks, four storehouses, along with a bakery and powder magazine.

The southern side of the fort faces an area where the lake curves toward the west, just before the mouth of the La Chute River. Between the fort and the lake, on this south side, a small town of sorts sprang up to house workers and other military people. This area was also where the boats and canoes landed. This area was called the Lower Town and was surrounded by a palisade. To the west of the town, close to the mouth of the La Chute, was a redoubt (small auxiliary fort). Between the east wall and the lake were vegetable gardens, and south of those were several gun batteries. Very near the point of the peninsula were the hospital and another storehouse. Finally by the beginning of 1758, the fort was mostly completed, with the exception of adding more stone to the face of the walls.

MONTCALM ARRIVES

Fort Carillon (we will call it that during the French period) was garrisoned throughout 1757 and was the launching point for the attack on Fort William Henry at the foot of Lake George. In August 1757, the French general in charge, Louis-Joseph de Montcalm (making his headquarters at Fort Carillon), captured Fort William Henry. This and several other French victories in 1757 induced the English to plan an attack on Fort Carillon scheduled for summer 1758.

BRITISH DISASTER

General James Abercromby was placed in charge of the English campaign. In June 1758 he had amassed a force of 17,000 troops near the remnants of Fort William Henry and in early July began moving (on Lake George) this large force north toward Ticonderoga. On July 6 Abercromby's forces landed near the La Chute River, about four miles from Fort Carillon. For some reason, still debated, the English did not attack immediately (on July 6), but instead waited a day and made their advance on the French July 7. This allowed the French to build entrenchments and a log wall about a half mile to the west of the fort, which allowed them to block the route to the fort. They constructed a nearly impenetrable abatis (felled trees with sharpened sticks pointing outward) just beyond their trenches.

The next day, July 8, 1758, Abercromby ordered a frontal assault on the French positions. The English had 17,000 troops, and the French defenders had only four thousand troops, which may have been a partial factor among the complex reasons that Abercromby failed to utilize his cannons. In spite of the numerical superiority, the assault was a disaster for the English. Wave after wave of brave English soldiers threw themselves against the French lines, only to be repulsed every time. At the end of the day the French entrenchments had not been breached, the fort was still French, and the English had suffered a staggering two thousand casualties. Abercromby and his men retreated back to their boats and then all the way down Lake George to Fort William Henry. This battle is referred to as the Battle of Carillon. Fort Carillon saw no more action in 1758.

BRITISH CAPTURE FORT TICONDEROGA

The year 1759 brought significant military success for the British in North America. In fact the French were pulling back their forces in order to defend the heart of New France along the St. Lawrence River. General Montcalm had left a small token force in Fort Carillon. In July 1759, General Jeffrey Amherst captured the fort without having to fire a shot, although the fleeing French troops did manage to blow up the powder magazine. This was the last significant action that the fort (we'll call it by the British name now, Fort Ticonderoga) saw during the French and Indian war, which ended officially in 1763 with the signing of the Treaty of Paris.

The English maintained a small garrison at Fort Ticonderoga through the postwar years, but it fell into significant disrepair.

REVOLUTION AND CAPTURE BY THE AMERICANS

The American Revolutionary War began in 1775. Fort Ticonderoga, though manned by only forty-eight soldiers was still very useful to the British as a supply depot and communications link between Canada and New York. On May 10, 1775, Ethan Allen and Benedict Arnold led a small force of "green Mountain Boys" and militia volunteers on a surprise attack of the fort. The surprise was complete; the fort and its contents were captured. Especially important were the cannons and also beneficial was the fact that British communications were disrupted. Ticonderoga's cannons proved very useful to General George Washington who was besieging Boston later that year. Washington sent Henry Knox to Fort Ticonderoga to bring back the cannons to Boston. Knox completed this challenging task successfully, and the cannons played an important role in ending the siege in Boston, eventually forcing the English to retreat to Halifax, Nova Scotia (March 1776).

Benedict Arnold was placed in command of Fort Ticonderoga after its capture by the Americans in May 1775. Later that year, in June, Arnold was unexpectedly replaced by Benjamin Hinman leading a force of over one thousand Connecticut Militia. This irritated Arnold greatly because he had never been notified about the change until Hinman showed up to take over. After Hinman took over, the fort was used as a staging area for an assault on Quebec City led by Philip Schuyler and Richard Montgomery. In May 1776 the British broke the siege of Quebec and pursued the American army all the way back to Fort Ticonderoga. In October 1776, on Lake Champlain, the British Navy defeated a hastily constructed American Navy, led by Benedict Arnold, in the hard-fought Battle of Valcour Island.

There were no more major actions at Fort Ticonderoga through the rest of 1776, although the Americans did significantly fortify their defenses there.

Early 1777 found some of the American generals discussing strategies to defeat an expected British incursion from the north, along the Champlain-Hudson River corridor. General Schuyler, now in charge of the forces at Ticonderoga, requested ten thousand troops to guard the fort. General Washington, believing the British would avoid Fort Ticonderoga, turned Schuyler's request down. The fort was then left garrisoned by General St. Clair with a force of only two thousand men, not enough to stop the British if they did attack the fort (which, of course, they proceeded to do).

BURGOYNE RECAPTURES THE FORT

British General John Burgoyne and his forces were on their way south with an eventual goal of joining up with other British forces in the Albany area. They arrived at Fort Ticonderoga in late June 1777 and, contrary to what General Washington had expected, proceeded to prepare a siege of Fort Ticonderoga. Burgoyne ordered his men to haul cannons up to the top of Mount Defiance, which overlooked the fort. This made Fort Ticonderoga untenable, and on July 5, 1777, St. Clair ordered the fort to be abandoned. Burgoyne and his men moved in the next day. The abandonment of supposedly impregnable Fort Ticonderoga, by General St. Clair, caused considerable distress throughout the colonies, including with General Washington.

As Burgoyne again headed south toward Albany (he would never make it; see chapter on Battles of Saratoga), he left seven hundred soldiers behind to man Fort Ticonderoga and its surrounding defenses. General Washington ordered General Benjamin Lincoln into nearby Vermont to harass the British and free American prisoners wherever possible. General Lincoln ordered Colonel John Brown to the Ticonderoga peninsula to release prisoners in the area and attack Fort Ticonderoga if he thought he could be successful. Brown wisely did not attempt to push the British out of the fort but did manage to free many Americans prisoners in the area.

General Burgoyne, meanwhile, ran into generals Horatio Gates and Benedict Arnold at Saratoga, New York. After two battles there, Burgoyne was forced to surrender his entire command to Gates in a stunning American victory, with worldwide repercussions. In November 1777, the British abandoned Fort Crown Point and Fort Ticonderoga, after destroying as much of the forts as they could. Fort Ticonderoga was occasionally used by transient British raiding parties until 1781 when the British surrendered all their forces to General Washington at Yorktown. After the war, Fort Ticonderoga was abandoned for military purposes and fell into disrepair from neglect.

RESTORATION

In 1785 Fort Ticonderoga and the surrounding lands became the property of New York State, which donated the property to Columbia and Union Colleges in 1803. William Ferris Pell bought the property in 1820. At first the property was used as a summer retreat. Thankfully the Pell family had a great sense of history and preservation. In 1909 the fort itself was restored and opened to the public. Stephen Hyatt Pell founded the Fort Ticonderoga Association, in 1931, which is now responsible for the fort and which has acquired historically important surrounding lands.

It should be noted that while a few of the cannon currently found in the fort are original to the site, the vast majority were collected from a variety of nations during the twentieth century restoration efforts, and their vintage spans the late seventeenth through the early nineteenth centuries.

Americans should be grateful to the Pell family for preserving this treasure and making it available to educate, fascinate, and thrill visitors.

X.

Crown Point State Historic Site

(And Fort St. Frederick National Historic Landmark)

Ruins of Fort at Crown Point. Photo by Barbara Hunt

Location: 21 Grandview Drive, Crown Point, Essex County, NY
12928

Directions: From points south, get on route NY 9N and head
north. Keep heading north (route stays NY 9N and NY 22N)
or Scenic NY 9N. Watch for and follow signs for Bridge to
Vermont route NY 185E (Bridge Road). Go about three and
one-half miles. Turn left into Crown Point State Historic Site.
From points north, proceed south on NY 9N until you reach
NY 185E (look for sign for Bridge to Vermont), turn left (east),
and proceed three and one-half miles as above.

Coordinates: 44.024853 N, -73.424377 W

Season: Mid-May through the end of October. Open Thursday to
Monday 9:30 am – 5:00 pm

Admission: Small fee to enter the museum (worth it). Children under
twelve free. Student discount. No fee to walk the grounds.

Note: Dogs allowed only on a short leash.

Contact: 21 Grandview Drive, Crown Point, NY 12928
Phone: (518)597-4666 or (518)597-3666
Web: www.nysparks.com/historicsites/34/details.aspx

DESCRIPTION

Crown Point State Historic Site preserves the ruins of one of the
finest and most important examples of eighteenth century military
engineering in North America, Fort Crown Point. It also preserves
the ruins of an earlier French fort named Fort St. Frederick, and
part of the French (and later English) villages that grew up outside
the forts.

Construction of Fort Crown Point began in 1760 but was never
finished partly due to a disastrous fire and explosion which destroyed
a large part of it in 1773. The historic site preserves what remains of
the fort in its 1773 condition, with the exception of the more recent
shoring up of some of the barrack's walls. Two of the barracks' stone
frames and part of a third one are still standing just as they appeared

in 1773, as are some of the fireplaces. A one-half-mile circumference dry moat (still visible) surrounds the fort. Just inside the moat are the ramparts (reinforced walls). These are twenty-five feet thick and more than twenty feet high. They were constructed of the material which was dug out of the ground while creating the moat. There are also five bastions (pointed projections from the ramparts to allow parallel firing along the walls) extending from the corners of the fort. All of these earthworks are still visible today (some of which can be seen on the park road as one drives into the site), though they are covered now by trees, brush, and grass.

FORT POINT A LA CHEVELURE AND
FORT ST. FREDERICK

Fort Crown Point was actually the third fort located in the area to take advantage of the narrowing of Lake Champlain due to the Crown Point Peninsula. In the early 1700s the French had built a very small fort just across the lake from Crown Point on Chimney Point. This was called Fort Point a la Chevelure. It was very small and was garrisoned by only a few French soldiers. In1731 the French were forced out of the Chimney Point fort by Massachusetts Militia. The French then moved across the lake to build the much larger Fort St. Frederick on Crown Point. Fort St. Frederick was built of black lime slate, with twenty feet thick walls, all of which was enclosed by a stone ditch. It included a three-story octagonal tower, stone barracks, and a fortified stone windmill (which was outside the walls to the east). Fort St. Frederic was garrisoned by one hundred French soldiers and was used extensively by the French and their Indian allies to stage raids on English settlements to the south and east. The fort was destroyed by the French in 1759 during the French and Indian war in order to avoid its being used by the rapidly advancing British forces. The ruins (parts of the foundation are still visible) of Fort St. Frederick are preserved by the State Historic Site and are found adjacent to the northeast corner of Fort Crown Point.

The Fort Crown Point State Historic Site visitors' center displays artifacts from, and tells the story of the forts and their French,

English, and American occupiers. There is ample parking at the site and the fort is "walk-able." There is even an occasional appearance from George Washington himself, looking over the defensive works from the back of his horse. This is a marvelous and very important historic site.

BRIEF HISTORY

GEOGRAPHY

It is said that the three most important factors in real estate are location, location, and location. The same can be said for military defensive works, especially in colonial times. The Crown Point Peninsula is and was a great location for a fort because of its nearness to the narrowest gap on Lake Champlain. Travel in the eighteenth century was most efficient by water, and Lake Champlain was part of a vast waterway that led from New York City into Canada. A canoe could travel up the Hudson River, take a short portage to Lake George, then paddle into Lake Champlain, and finally travel up the Richelieu River into Canada. A few guns at the Crown Point Peninsula (where Lake Champlain is less than one-half mile wide) could control lake traffic in either direction. This area, important for thousands of years to Native Americans, was especially important at this time in history because the French to the north, in present-day Canada, and the British to the south and east, were in conflict over control of North America. This water route was heavily used especially by the French and their Indian allies to attack English settlements to the south and east.

The French were the first of the European powers to recognize the strategic value of a fort on the Crown Point Peninsula and do something about it. The French first built a fort in 1726 on Chimney Point (the point on the east [Vermont] side of the lake across from Crown Point). This early fort, called Fort Point a la Chevelure, was very small, about fifty feet square (fifty feet per side) and was garrisoned by just twenty French soldiers. The French and their native allies used this area to stage their raids on the English settlements.

In 1731 the French were driven out of Fort Point a la Chevelure by Massachusetts Militia. The French crossed Lake Champlain into New York Province, and the Massachusetts Militia did not follow.

FORT ST. FREDERICK IS ERECTED

Next the French decided to erect a larger and more substantial fort on the Crown Point Peninsula in order to maximize their ability to control lake traffic and, as before, a place from which to stage raids on English settlements. The man in charge was Sieur de la Fresniere. Fresniere built the fort using black lime slate which was locally available. The fort was erected very close to the water. It was star shaped with five points. The substantial ramparts were twenty feet high and twenty feet thick and were enclosed by a ditch. Inside the fort were stone barracks for officers and enlisted troops, as well as a small church to serve the men's spiritual side.

A three-story watch tower was erected on the northwest corner of the fort. The tower was built using the same black slate used in the fort's walls and was considered "bomb proof." It mounted several cannons as well as smaller guns. Just east of the fort, on a small point that jutted out into the lake, the men erected a fortified windmill to serve as a lookout.

Approximately ten miles to the south of Fort St. Frederick, at the bottom of Lake Champlain, is another area which would lend itself to a defensive work with the idea of controlling lake traffic. That area is the Ticonderoga peninsula, and this was where the French began building Fort Carillon in 1755. Even before Fort carillon was built the French had established a military road from Crown Point to Ticonderoga. This road ran along the west shore of the lake, about 350 yards from the water. After Fort St. Frederick established its protective presence, a French village grew up outside the fort and along this military road. The village seems to have been somewhat scattered along the road and consisted mostly of farms and houses.

With the completion of Fort St. Frederick in the early 1730s, the French now had a place to block all enemy boat traffic up Lake Champlain. Quite regularly for more than twenty years the French and their Indian allies used the fort as a place to rendezvous and launch brutal raids against the English settlements of New York and New England.

THE FRENCH AND INDIAN WAR BEGINS

May 28, 1754, Lieutenant Colonel George Washington along with his small party of Virginia Militia and a few Mingo warriors attacked a French scouting party in Jumonville Glen (in current-day Pennsylvania) signaling the beginning of the French and Indian War, and the beginning of the end for French presence in North America. During the war, Fort St. Frederick continued as a very important base of operations for the French until 1759. That year British General Sir Jeffery Amherst, after capturing Fort Ticonderoga (Fort Carillon), began advancing on Fort St. Frederick. To prevent the English from utilizing the fort to their benefit, the French destroyed Fort St. Frederick and fled north into Canada.

FORT CROWN POINT

The year 1759 marked the beginning of a positive trend for British forces and the beginning of the end of French victories in the French and Indian War. The previous year, 1758, had seen a disastrous attack by the British on Fort Carillon, ten miles to the south of Fort St. Frederick. The British, led by General Abercrombie, had suffered huge losses and failed to capture the fort. However, in 1759 the British, now led by the more able General Jeffery Amherst, captured the damaged Fort Carillon (which they called Fort Ticonderoga) on July 31 as the French fled north toward Crown Point. Amherst spent a few days repairing the damage done to the fort by the fleeing French forces and then moved north with the intention of capturing Fort St. Frederick. In August the French, knowing that the British were on the way, blew up Fort St. Frederick and fled farther north toward Canada. General Amherst upon reaching Fort St. Frederick could see that the smallish fort was beyond repair and decided to build a much larger fort on high ground two hundred yards directly southwest of the ruins of Fort St. Frederick. This new fort would be called His Majesty's Fort at Crown Point (sometimes referred to as Fort Amherst).

Construction of Fort Crown Point was begun in the late summer of 1759. The design of the huge fort was based on the system of fortifications put forth by a great French military engineer named the Marquis de Vauban. At times there were as many as three thousand men working on the fort. A large moat was dug out of the limestone bedrock by the soldiers. The dirt and rock which were removed in the process were then used to build twenty-five-foot-thick ramparts, which were also twenty-five feet high and faced with masonry. The circumference of the moat was one-half mile, and the heart of the fort contained more than six-and-one-half acres. Five bastions extending out made the shape of the fort a star. The men also built three redoubts (small mini-forts), several blockhouses and military roads. The resulting fort was three times larger than Fort Ticonderoga.

Just outside the walls of the fort a small village grew up, consisting of some soldiers' homes, a small store, and a tavern.

For the decade after the end of the French and Indian War in (officially in 1763), Fort Crown Point served mainly as storage depot for artillery pieces and other military stores.

DISASTER AT CROWN POINT

In 1773 a disastrous fire broke out in Fort Crown Point. Unfortunately the fire reached the powder magazine and a large explosion ensued. Damage was very extensive; the fire and explosion damaged much of the interior of the fort save for the stone walls of two of the barracks. British military engineers began making plans to rebuild the fort, but before they could begin reconstruction the Revolutionary War broke out. Meanwhile much of the artillery and most of the British soldiers had been moved to Fort Ticonderoga leaving just a few soldiers to guard Fort Crown Point.

REVOLUTIONARY WAR

By 1775 the Americans and British were actively fighting each other in the Revolutionary War. In May of that year American Colonel Seth Warner with fifty of the "Green Mountain boys" captured Fort Crown Point and its small garrison of about ten soldiers. At this time, General Washington besieging Boston, ordered Henry Knox to go to Ticonderoga and procure cannon for the American cause. Earlier many of the more than one hundred cannons originally at Fort Crown Point had been moved to Fort Ticonderoga and now Knox moved them (on sleds) to the Boston area for use by General Washington in evicting the British from that city.

General Washington and the Continental Congress along with other American military leaders (including the brilliant General Benedict Arnold) soon decided that as part of their strategy to defeat the British, they would plan an invasion of British Canada to be led by General Montgomery and General Arnold. Fort Crown Point now in American hands served as a staging area for the eventually unsuccessful attack on Canada late in that year (1775).

The year 1776 found the British building a navy on Lake Champlain, thus threatening all the Patriot positions in the area. To counter this threat the Americans built a navy of their own on the southern portion of the lake and placed General Arnold in charge of it. Arnold used Fort Crown Point as a staging area for his Lake Champlain naval campaign. Unfortunately for the Americans, Arnold's navy was destroyed by the British in 1776 during the Battle of Valcour Island, despite a heroic effort on the part of Arnold and his sailors.

THE BRITISH CAPTURE CROWN POINT

The year after the American defeat at Valcour Island, 1777, the British Army under General "Gentleman Johnny" Burgoyne began an invasion of the American colonies from Canada. As the British approached Fort Crown Point, the Americans abandoned it and fled south.

General Burgoyne used Crown Point as a supply depot and hospital. As Burgoyne moved south toward Fort Ticonderoga, he left a small force of two hundred soldiers at Crown Point. Burgoyne was eventually defeated in the remarkable Battles of Saratoga, but the British retained control of Fort Crown Point until the end of the Revolutionary War in 1783. The fort was then abandoned forever with regard to active military uses.

NEW YORK STATE PRESERVES A TREASURE

New York State acquired the sites of both Fort St. Frederick and Fort Crown Point in the early 1900s. They are administered as Crown Point State Historic Site, though the state property extends beyond the grounds of the forts. Currently there is a state campground near the lake and even a statue of Samuel de Champlain erected over the site of Fort St. Frederick's windmill. Fort Crown Point was declared a national historic landmark in 1968. What a thrill it is to be able to visit the ruins of these two remarkable historic forts. It is easy to picture in one's mind the energetic activity of the French, English, Americans, and Indians on a site once valued so much for its location, location, and location.

Sources

This book should be viewed as a detailed historic site guidebook and not necessarily as a history book. In preparing this book we have relied heavily on the World Wide Web. The Web is an amazing source of information. Research, using the Web, can be accomplished quicker and less expensively than ever before. Individual Web pages utilized will be listed, by chapter, below. All pages used in this book have been accessed between November 2011 and March 2014. Following are some useful general sites we have used for historic site information.

For information on nearly any topic, the Wikipedia Web site is a good place to start. Information at Wikipedia is somewhat brief, but pages usually have links to more pages on the topic being addressed. A subdivision of Wikipedia is FortWiki.com which focuses specifically on United States and Canadian forts and is very useful for history-oriented users. For detailed information on many historic sites, check the National Registry of Historic Sites at http://1.usa.gov/12kafDX. While difficult to use, it has detailed and useful historic information including an inventory document containing very detailed description of the current site and its history.

The state of New York also has some useful Web sites. The New York Department of Parks (http://www.nysparks.com/historic-sites) is a great place search for historic sites and especially to get historic site logistic information (hours, fees, addresses, etc.). Just type in the site you wish to find in the search box or pick one from a drop-down box.

Specific North American fort information including a short summary and useful links is available at www.northamericanforts. com.

Some of New York's historic sites have affiliated nongovernment organizations that have helpful Web sites. Often these are called "Friends of" the site name, for example, "Friends of Johnson Hall" (http://www.friendsofjohnsonhall.org/jhall.html).

The map is from a US Government Web site with various maps of all fifty states.http://nationalatlas.gov/printable/images/pdf/reference/pagegen_ny.pdf.

Introduction

Cohen, Eliot, A. Conquered Into Liberty. New York. Free Press (Simon & Shuster, Inc.). 2011.

Kammen, Michael. Colonial New York - A History. New York. Oxford University Press.1975.

Beauchamp, William M (S.T.D.). History of the New York Iroquois. New York State Education Department. 1905.

Parkman, Francis. France and England in North America—Volume I. New York, N.Y.: Library Classics of the United States, Inc. 1963.

Clark, Charles E. The Eastern Frontier. New York. University Press of New England. 1970.

http://www.canals.ny.gov/history/history.html. Great New York State site for excellent Erie Canal history.

http://en.wikipedia.org/wiki/Erie_Canal. Good Wiki summary Erie Canal.

http://en.wikipedia.org/wiki/History_of_New_York. Excellent New York State History going back to 10000 years ago.

http://www.tolatsga.org/iro.html. Great site for detailed Iroquois history.

http://en.wikipedia.org/wiki/Iroquois. Wiki's Iroquois summary.

http://nativeamericanencyclopedia.com/iroquois-culture/. Iroquois culture.

http://eriecanal.org/. Interesting Erie Canal information.
http://en.wikipedia.org/wiki/Upstate_New_York. Wiki on Upstate New York.

Chapter I. "Old" Fort Niagara

http://en.wikipedia.org/wiki/Battle_of_Fort_Niagara. Wiki on the successful siege of Fort Niagara by the British in the F&I War.
http://dmna.ny.gov/forts/fortsM_P/niagaraFort.htm. NYS Military Museum info on Fort Niagara.
http://fortwiki.com/Fort_Niagara. Fort Wiki. Basics.
http://en.wikipedia.org/wiki/Fort_Niagara?oldid=. Wiki's take. Nice.
http://www.oldfortniagara.org/. Fort Web Site.
http://www.nysparks.com/historic-sites/31/details.aspx. State site.
http://pdfhost.focus.nps.gov/docs/NHLS/Text/66000556.pdf. National Historic Landmark nomination form. Very detailed site inventory and history.
http://en.wikipedia.org/wiki/Battle_of_La_Belle-Famille. Wiki on Battle of La Belle Famille.
Parkman, Francis. Montcalm and Wolfe. New York, N.Y., Atheneum. 1984. (originally printed 1884),

Chapter II. Fort Ontario

http://fortwiki.com/Fort_Ontario. Fort Wiki site, photos and summary.
http://www.nysparks.com/historic-sites/20/details.aspx. New York Parks Web site on Fort Ontario.
http://fortontario.com/. Friends of Fort Ontario. Good information.
http://en.wikipedia.org/wiki/Fort_Ontario. Wiki's site.
http://www.revolutionaryday.com/nyroute5/ftontario/default.htm. Good history.
http://www.oswegony.org/ABOUT_fort.html. City of Oswego info on the fort.
Parkman, Francis. Montcalm and Wolfe. New York, N.Y., Atheneum. 1984. (originally printed 1884),

Chapter III. Erie Canal State Historic Park

http://eriecanal.org/OECSHP.html. Basic and detailed canal park and history.

http://www.nycanals.com/Old_Erie_Canal_State_Historic_Park. Excellent up to date details about the park.

http://www.nysparks.com/parks/17/details.aspx. New York State Parks dept page for OECSHP.

http://en.wikipedia.org/wiki/Old_Erie_Canal_State_Historic_Park. Wiki's page brief but with a few good links.

http://eriecanal.org/index.html. Good site on Erie Canal.

http://www.eriecanalvillage.net/. Erie Canal Village home page.

http://clcbm.org/. Chittenango Landing Boat Museum home page.

Chapter IV. Fort Stanwix

Dupuy, R. Ernest and Trevor N., The Compact History of the Revolutionary War. New York. Hawthorn Books Inc., 1963,

Beauchamp, William M (S.T.D.). History of the New York Iroquois. New York State Education Department. 1905.

Kammen, Michael. Colonial New York - A History. New York. Oxford University Press.1975. PP 372–273.

Greenwood, Richard. (Historian, Landmark Review Task Force). National Register of Historic Places Inventory – Nomination Form. United States Department of the Interior, National Park Service. 1976. (This is a detailed survey and history of the site performed by the US Government as part of the Historic Landmark process.)

http://militaryhistory.about.com/od/AmRev1777/p/American-Revolution-Battle-Of-Oriskany.htm.

http://www.nysparks.com/historic-sites/21/details.aspx.

http://theamericanrevolution.org/battledetail.aspx?battle=18.

http://home.nps.gov/fost/historyculture/the-battle-at-oriska.htm.

http://www.nps.gov/nr/twhp/wwwlps/lessons/79oriskany/79facts2.htm.

Chapter V. Oriskany Battlefield State Historic Site

http://militaryhistory.about.com/od/AmRev1777/p/American-Revolution-Battle-Of-Oriskany.htm. Good account of the battle.

http://en.wikipedia.org/wiki/Battle_of_Oriskany. Wiki version. Excellent.

http://pdfhost.focus.nps.gov/docs/NHLS/Text/66000558.pdf. Government NHL nomination form. Great description and detail.

http://www.nysparks.com/historic-sites/21/details.aspx. NYS Parks basics.

http://theamericanrevolution.org/battledetail.aspx?battle=18. Useful summary version.

http://home.nps.gov/fost/historyculture/the-battle-at-oriska.htm. Great version by National Park Service.

http://www.nps.gov/nr/twhp/wwwlps/lessons/79oriskany/79facts2.htm. Another page from NPS on battle. Good synopsis.

Chapter VI. Johnson Hall

Parkman, Francis. Montcalm and Wolfe. New York, N.Y., Atheneum. 1984. (originally printed 1884),

http://pdfhost.focus.nps.gov/docs/NHLS/Text/66000520.pdf. Federal Government National Historic Landmark nomination form. Very detailed.

http://www.nysparks.com/historic-sites/10/details.aspx. New York State Parks page re Johnson Hall.

http://en.wikipedia.org/wiki/Johnson_Hall. Wiki page on the Hall.

http://www.friendsofjohnsonhall.org/jhall.html. Friends of Johnson Hall. Well done.

Chapter VII. Fort William Henry Restoration and Museum

Parkman, Francis. Montcalm and Wolfe. New York, N.Y., Atheneum. 1984. (originally printed 1884),

http://en.wikipedia.org/wiki/Fort_William_Henry. Wiki.

http://fortwiki.com/Fort_William_Henry_%283%29. Fort Wiki. Very good map, photos.

http://www.fwhmuseum.com/. Museum's home page.

http://militaryhistory.about.com/od/battleswars16011800/p/lake-george.htm. Good summary of the fort history.

http://en.wikipedia.org/wiki/Battle_of_Lake_George. Wiki's account of the Battle of Lake George.

Cohen, Eliot, A. Conquered Into Liberty. New York. Free Press (Simon & Shuster, Inc.). 2011.

Chapter VIII. Saratoga National Historical

Dupuy, R. Ernest and Trevor N., The Compact History of the Revolutionary War. New York. Hawthorn Books Inc., 1963,

http://en.wikipedia.org/wiki/Battle_of_Saratoga. Wiki's version of the Battles.

http://www.revolutionaryday.com/usroute4/saratoga/default.htm. Really well done tour of the battlefield.

http://www.nps.gov/sara/index.htm. National Park service site.

http://en.wikipedia.org/wiki/Saratoga_National_Historical_Park. Wiki's page about the park itself.

http://www.nps.gov/history/NR/twhp/wwwlps/lessons/93saratoga/93saratoga.htm. National Park Service lessons about the battles.

http://www.nps.gov/history/NR/twhp/wwwlps/lessons/93saratoga/93locate1.htm. nice NPS map of overall campaign.

http://battle1777.saratoga.org/images-page/map_park.jpg. Nice map of Park.

Chapter IX. Fort Ticonderoga

Parkman, Francis. Montcalm and Wolfe. New York, N.Y., Atheneum. 1984. (originally printed 1884),

http://en.wikipedia.org/wiki/Fort_Ticonderoga. Wiki site. Extensively covers the fort's history.

http://www.fortticonderoga.org/visit/hours. The fort's Web site. Comprehensive and well done.

http://www.historiclakes.org/Ticonderoga/Ticonderoga.html. Nice concise version.

http://fortwiki.com/Fort_Ticonderoga. Good summary. Great photos.

Cohen, Eliot, A. Conquered Into Liberty. New York. Free Press (Simon & Shuster, Inc.). 2011.

Dupuy, R. Ernest and Trevor N., The Compact History of the Revolutionary War. New York. Hawthorn Books Inc., 1963,

Chapter X. Fort Crown Point State Historic Site

http://pdfhost.focus.nps.gov/docs/NHLS/Text/66000517.pdf. National Historic Landmark nomination form. Very detailed inventory and history for Fort St Frederick.

http://pdfhost.focus.nps.gov/docs/NHLS/Text/68000033.pdf. Gov survey form, Crown Point. Great detail..

http://www.nysparks.com/historic-sites/34/details.aspx. State Parks Web Page.

http://fortwiki.com/Fort_Crown_Point. Fort Wiki version Great old map and pics.

http://en.wikipedia.org/wiki/Fort_Crown_Point. Wiki's version.

http://en.wikipedia.org/wiki/Fort_St._Fr%C3%A9d%C3%A9ric. Wiki fort St. Frederick.

http://fortwiki.com/Fort_St._Frederic. Fort Wiki on Fort St Frederick.

http://www.saratogaassociates.com/historic-fort-st-frederic/. Fantastic animation of fort St Frederick

Cohen, Eliot, A. Conquered Into Liberty. New York. Free Press (Simon & Shuster), 2011. Index

Index

A

Abercromby, James (General) 103
Albany 16, 17, 18, 28, 36, 52, 55, 60,
    61, 71, 78, 90, 91, 92, 93, 105
Algonquian 15, 16, 17, 100
American Revolution 14, 36, 51, 58
Amherst, Jeffery (General) 112
Arnold, Benedict 18, 55, 66, 91, 93,
    94, 95, 104, 106, 114

B

Barge Canal 43, 46
Baron de Dieskau 72
Battle of Lake George 72, 79, 122
battles of Saratoga 18, 55, 58, 59, 60,
    66, 87, 89, 92, 93, 95, 105,
    115
Bemis Heights 92
Brant, Joseph 36, 53, 61, 63
Breymann's redoubt 94
Brown Bess 23
Burgoyne, John (General) 18, 36, 52,
    53, 55, 59, 60, 61, 66, 89, 90,
    91, 92, 93, 94, 95, 105, 106,
    114, 115

C

Carillon Battlefield 98
Castle 16, 21, 23, 25, 29
Champlain 16, 17, 36, 52, 60, 78, 79,
    90, 98, 99, 100, 101, 104, 105,
    109, 110, 111, 114, 115
chateau 23, 25
Chittenango Landing Canal Boat Mu-
    seum 39, 40, 41, 42, 43
Civil War 14, 26, 28, 38
Clinton, DeWitt 45
Cooper, James Fennimore 76, 77

D

de Lery, Chaussegros 23
de Montcalm, Marquis (General) 35,
    76, 81
Denonville (French governor) 25
de Verrazano, Giovanni 16

E

Erie Canal 4, 5, 18, 19, 28, 39, 40,
    41, 42, 43, 44, 45, 46, 118,
    119, 120
Erie Canal Village 39, 40, 42, 43, 120

F

Fort Carillon 80, 101, 102, 103, 111,
    112
Fort Crown Point 60, 106, 108, 109,
    112, 113, 114, 115, 123
Fort Dayton 50, 54, 55, 62, 66
Fort Edward 72, 79, 81, 82, 83, 90
Fort Nassau 16
Fort Niagara 4, 5, 17, 21, 22, 23, 24,

25, 26, 27, 28, 29, 72, 119
Fort Ontario 4, 5, 31, 32, 33, 34, 35, 36, 37, 38, 119
Fort Orange 16
Fort Pepperell 34
Fort Point a la Chevelure 109, 110
Fort St. Frederick 72, 79, 80, 101, 107, 108, 109, 111, 112, 115
Fort Ticonderoga 4, 5, 9, 60, 80, 90, 91, 97, 98, 100, 101, 103, 104, 105, 106, 112, 113, 114, 115, 122
Fraser, Simon (General) 92, 94, 95
French and Indian War 13, 14, 17, 26, 27, 35, 49, 50, 51, 61, 72, 76, 77, 78, 80, 83, 112, 113
Fulton, Robert 18
fur trade 13, 24, 26, 28, 34, 68, 69, 70, 71

G

Gansevoort, Peter (Colonel) 52, 62
Gates, Horatio (General) 18, 52, 89, 92

H

Herkimer, Nicholas 54, 58, 62, 91
Howe, William (General) 60
Hudson, Henry 16
Hudson River 15, 16, 19, 28, 33, 36, 44, 50, 52, 55, 60, 61, 66, 78, 79, 85, 88, 90, 91, 92, 99, 105, 110

I

Iroquois 14, 15, 16, 17, 23, 24, 27, 51, 52, 53, 55, 61, 62, 71, 72, 73, 78, 99, 100, 118, 120
Iroquois Confederacy 15

J

Jogues, Isaac 100

Johnson, William (Sir) 27, 35, 51, 68, 70, 72, 73, 74

K

King George's War 14
King Phillip's War 13
King William's War 14
Knox, Henry 104, 114

L

LaSalle 25
Lignery (Captain) 27

M

Marquis de Vauban 113
Marquis de Vaudreuil 101
mercenaries 61
Militia 12, 36, 50, 54, 59, 66, 90, 104, 112
Mohawk 15, 16, 33, 36, 50, 51, 53, 55, 60, 61, 62, 68, 71, 72, 90, 100
Monro, George (Lieutenant Colonel) 80
Montcalm 81, 82, 83, 97, 102, 103, 119, 121, 122
Montreal 34, 78, 90
Morgan, Daniel 92, 94
Mount Defiance 98, 99, 105

N

National Park Service 9, 48, 49, 50, 56, 66, 85, 87, 120, 121, 122
Native Americans 14, 29, 35, 50, 63, 73, 74, 82, 99, 110
Natives 13
New York City 17, 18, 19, 28, 33, 45, 50, 52, 60, 90, 91, 93, 99, 110

O

Oneida 15, 33, 43, 50, 54, 59, 60,

61, 62
Oswego 4, 17, 31, 32, 33, 34, 35, 36,
    37, 38, 50, 52, 60, 61, 90, 91,
    119

P

Patriots 12, 59, 65, 66
Pontiac's Rebellion 35
Pouchot (Captain) 25, 27
Prideaux, John (Brigadier General) 27

Q

Quebec 17, 78, 104
Queen Anne's War 14

R

Regulars 12, 36, 62, 80
Revolutionary War 12, 17, 18, 28,
    36, 37, 49, 52, 55, 59, 62, 66,
    74, 87, 89, 101, 104, 113, 114,
    115, 120, 122, 123
Roger's Rangers 80
Rogers, Robert 79

S

Schuyler, Phillip (Major General) 51,
    55, 66, 88
Stanwix, John (General) 49, 50
St. Clair (General) 105
St. Laurence River 16
St. Leger 36, 52, 53, 54, 55, 56, 60,
    61, 62, 63, 65, 66, 90, 91
St. Leger, Barry (General) 36, 60

T

Tories 12
Treaty of Paris 13, 17, 72, 78, 104

W

War of 1812 14, 37
Washington, George (General) 12, 37,

49, 51, 52, 91, 100, 104, 105,
    106, 110, 112, 114
Weissenberg, Catherine 71
Willett Center 48, 49, 50
Willett, Marinus (Lieutenant Colonel)
    37, 53, 54, 65

About the Author

David MacNab has a BA degree in mathematics and a master's degree in education. He also has successfully completed all the coursework for a master's degree in computer science. He has utilized his education first working extensively as a social worker, followed by several decades as a computer database programmer. David also has had a lifelong passion for early American history, especially colonial times in northeast America, early settlements along the northern Atlantic coast of North America, and the century-long conflict between France and England for control of North America. His interests have taken him throughout New England, to Maritime Canada including Newfoundland, to the American West, to France, and down a portion of the Amazon River.

This is David's third book. His first book examined the drama and controversies of the Battle of the Little Bighorn, and his second book was a guide to fifteen interesting historic sites along the coast and rivers of Maine. David continues his career as a passionate student, author, and sometimes speaker of early northeast America topics.

Printed in the USA
CPSIA information can be obtained
at www.ICGtesting.com
LVHW061536280124
770160LV00050B/2567